A G
THAN NAPOLEON

SCIPIO AFRICANUS

BY

CAPTAIN B. H. LIDDELL HART

WITH FRONTISPIECE AND MAPS

BOSTON

LITTLE, BROWN, AND COMPANY

1927

PRINTED IN GREAT BRITAIN

From the bust in the Capitoline Museum, supposed to be
Scipio Africanus.

TO

THE MASTER, FELLOWS AND SCHOLARS

OF

CORPUS CHRISTI COLLEGE
CAMBRIDGE

PREFACE.

THE excuse for this book is that no recent biography of Scipio exists; the first and last in English appeared in 1817, and is the work of a country clergyman, who omits any study of Scipio as a soldier! The reason for this book is that, apart from the romance of Scipio's personality and his political importance as the founder of Rome's world-dominion, his military work has a greater value to modern students of war than that of any other great captain of the past. A bold claim, and yet its truth will, I hope, be substantiated in the following pages.

For the study of tactical methods the campaigns of Napoleon or of 1870, even of 1914-1918 perhaps, are as dead as those of the third century B.C. But the art of generalship does not age, and it is because Scipio's battles are richer in stratagems and ruses—many still feasible to-day—than those of any other commander in history that they are an unfailing object-lesson to soldiers.

Strategically Scipio is still more "modern." The present is a time of disillusionment, when we are realising that slaughter is not synonymous with victory, that the "destruction of the enemy's main armed forces on the battlefield" is at best but a means to the end, and not an end in itself, as the purblind apostles of Clausewitz had deceived themselves—and the world, unhappily. In the future, even more than in the past, the need is to study and understand the interplay of the military, economic, and political forces, which are inseparable in strategy. Because Scipio more than any other great captain understood and combined these forces in his strategy, despite the very "modern" handicap of being the servant of a republic—not, like Alexander, Frederick, Napoleon, a despot,—the study of his life is peculiarly apposite to-day. Above all, because the moral objective was the aim of all his plans, whether political, strategical, or tactical.

My grateful thanks are due to Sir Geoffrey Butler, K.B.E., M.P., Fellow of Corpus Christi College, Cambridge; to Mr W. E. Heitland, M.A., Fellow of St John's College, Cambridge; and to Mr E. G. Hawke, M.A., Lecturer at Queen's College, London, for their kindness in reading the proofs and for helpful comments.

B. H. L. H.

CONTENTS.

LIST OF MAPS.

The memory of a spectacular failure eclipses that of enduring success

A GREATER THAN NAPOLEON

SCIPIO AFRICANUS.

The road to failure is the road to fame

INTRODUCTION.

THE road to failure is the road to fame—such
apparently must be the verdict on posterity's
estimate of the world's greatest figures. The
flash of the meteor impresses the human imagina-
tion more than the remoter splendour of the
star, fixed immutably in the high heavens. Is
it that final swoop earthwards, the unearthly
radiance ending in the common dust, that, by
its evidence of the tangible or the finite, gives
to the meteor a more human appeal? So with
the luminaries of the human system, provided
that the ultimate fall has a dramatic note, the
memory of spectacular failure eclipses that of
enduring success. Again, it may be that the
completeness of his course lends individual em-
phasis to the great failure, throwing his work
into clearer relief, whereas the man whose

A

efforts are crowned with permanent success
builds a stepping-stone by which others may
advance still farther, and so merges his own
fame in that of his successors.

The theory at least finds ample confirmation
in the realm of action. A Napoleon and a Lee
are enshrined in drama, in novel, and in memoir
by the hundred. A Wellington and a Grant
are almost forgotten by the writers of the nations
they brought through peril intact and victorious.
Even a Lincoln may only have been saved from
comparative oblivion by the bullet of an assassin,
a Nelson by death in the hour of victory, which
relieved by emotion-awakening tragedy the dis-
repute of a successful end. It would seem likely
that a century hence the name of Ludendorff
will be emblazoned as the heroic figure of the
European War, while that of Foch sinks into
obscurity; there are signs already of this tendency to exalt the defeated.

For permanence of reputation a man of action
must appeal to emotion, not merely to the mind;
and since the living man himself no longer can
kindle the emotions of posterity, the dramatic
human touch of ultimate failure is essential.
This truth would seem to hold in most branches
of human effort. Scott's gallant but unavailing
attempt to reach the South Pole lives in the
world's memory, while the successful ventures

the glorification of dramatic failure at the expense of enduring achievement

of Amundsen and Peary are fading. In sport, Dorando's Marathon is an enduring memory; but who among the general public could recall the name of Hayes, the actual victor, or, indeed, that of any subsequent Marathon winner.

For this irrational, this sentimental verdict, it is fashionable to fix the blame on modern journalism, yet the barest survey of history shows that its origins lie far back in the mists of time. On the historian, in fact—who of all men should by training and outlook put his trust in reason—falls the major responsibility for this eternal tendency—the glorification of dramatic failure at the expense of enduring achievement. The history of the ancient confirms that of the modern world, and in no example more strikingly than that of Scipio Africanus, the subject of this brief study, which is an attempt to redress the "historical" balance by throwing further weights of knowledge and military appreciation on Scipio's side, not as commonly by detraction from his rivals. Gradually, progressively, the belittlement of Scipio has been pressed by historians anxious to enhance the fame of Hannibal. It is the more unreasonable, the less excusable, because here there are no mass of conflicting sources and contemporary opinions. The reliable data on which to base a study and a judgment are practically limited to the works of Polybius and Livy, with but a few grains from other, and admittedly less trustworthy, ancient authorities. And of these two, Polybius, the earlier, is almost contemporary with events, the friend of Gaius Lælius, Scipio's constant subordinate, from whom he could get first-hand evidence and judgments. He had the family archives of the Scipios at his disposal for research, and he had been over the actual battlefields while many of the combatants were still alive. Thus he gained an almost unique base upon which to form his estimate.

Further, being a Greek, his views are less suspect than those of Livy of being coloured by Roman patriotic bias, while modern historical criticism is unanimous in its tribute alike to his impartiality, his thoroughness of research, and the soundness of his critical insight.

The verdict of Polybius is clear, and his facts still more so.

That there were divergent judgments of Scipio among the Romans of succeeding generations is true; but Polybius explains the reasons so convincingly, their truth borne out by the known facts of Scipio's strategical and tactical plans, that there is no vestige of excuse for modern writers to regard as due to luck what superstition led the ancients to ascribe to divine aid.

what is praiseworthy belongs only to men of sound judgment and mental ability

INTRODUCTION

"The fact that he was almost the most famous man of all time makes every one desirous to know what sort of man he was, and what were the natural gifts and the training which enabled him to accomplish so many great actions. But none can help falling into error and acquiring a mistaken impression of him, as the estimate of those who have given us their views about him is very wide of the truth." ". . . They represent him as a man favoured by fortune . . . such men being, in their opinion, more divine and more worthy of admiration than those who always act by calculation. They are not aware that the one deserves praise and the other only congratulation, being common to ordinary men, whereas what is praiseworthy belongs only to men of sound judgment and mental ability, whom we should consider to be the most divine and most beloved by the gods. To me it seems that the character and principles of Scipio much resembled those of Lycurgus, the Lacedæmonian legislator. For neither must we suppose that Lycurgus drew up the constitution of Sparta under the influence of superstition and solely prompted by the Pythia, nor that Scipio won such an empire for his country by following the suggestion of dreams and omens. But since both of them saw that most men neither readily accept any-

thing unfamiliar to them, nor venture on great
risks without the hope of divine help, Lycurgus
made his own scheme more acceptable and more
easily believed in by invoking the oracles of the
Pythia in support of projects due to himself,
while Scipio similarly made the men under his
command more sanguine and more ready to face
perilous enterprises by instilling into them the
belief that his projects were divinely inspired.
But that he invariably acted on calculation and
foresight, and that the successful issue of his
plans was always in accord with rational ex-
pectation, will be evident."

To the mind of to-day not only does such an
explanation appear inherently probable, but
affords a key to the understanding of a man
whose triumphs, whether military, political, or
diplomatic, were, above all, due to his supreme
insight into the psychology of men. Who,
moreover, applied this gift like the conductor
of a great orchestra to the production of a world
harmony. In conducting policy, through war
to peace, he indeed attained a concord which
aptly fulfilled the musical definition: "A combination which both by its . . . smoothness and
by its logical origin and purpose in the scheme
can form a point of repose." As a conductor of
the human orchestra he had, however, two
weaknesses, one inborn and one developing with

years. He could not comprehend the low notes
—the narrowness and baseness to which men
can descend,—and the exaltation of spirit born
of his power over men prevented him from
hearing the first warnings of that discord which
was to impair the glorious symphony so nearly
completed.

CHAPTER I.

HALF LIGHT.

PUBLIUS CORNELIUS SCIPIO was born at Rome in the 517th year from the city's foundation— 235 B.C. Though a member of one of the most illustrious and ancient families, the Cornelii, of his early years and education no record, not even an anecdote, has come down to us. Indeed, not until he is chosen, through a combination of circumstances and his own initiative, to command the army in Spain at the age of twenty-four, does history give us more than an occasional fleeting glimpse of his progress. Yet bare and brief as these are, each is significant. The first is at the battle of the Ticinus, Hannibal's initial encounter with the Roman arms on Italian soil, after his famous passage of the Alps. Here the youthful Scipio, a lad of seventeen, accompanied his father, the Roman commander. If his first experience of battle was on the losing side, he at least emerged with enviable distinction. Let the story be told in

Polybius's words : "His father had placed him in command of a picked troop of horse " (in reserve on a small hill) "in order to ensure his safety ; but when he caught sight of his father in the battle, surrounded by the enemy and escorted only by two or three horsemen and dangerously wounded, he at first endeavoured to urge those with him to go to the rescue, but when they hung back for a time owing to the large numbers of the enemy round them, he is said with reckless daring to have charged the encircling force alone. Upon the rest being now forced to attack, the enemy were terror-struck and broke up, and Publius Scipio, thus unexpectedly rescued, was the first to salute his son as his deliverer." It is said that the consul ordered a civic crown, the Roman V.C., to be presented to his son, who refused it, saying that "the action was one that rewarded itself." The exploit does credit to the young Scipio's gallantry, but the outcome, as emphasised by Polybius, does still more credit to his psychological insight. "Having by this service won a universally acknowledged reputation for bravery, he in subsequent times refrained from exposing his person without sufficient reason when his country reposed her hopes of success on him—conduct characteristic not of a commander who relies on luck, but on one gifted with intelligence."

To the present generation, with personal experience of war, the point may have greater force than to the closeted historians. To the former, the higher commander who aspires to be a platoon leader, thrusting himself into the fight at the expense of his proper duty of direction, is not the heroic or inspired figure that he appears to the civilian. To some too, not natural lovers of danger for its own sake—and these are rare in any army,—the point will touch a chord of memory, reminding them of how by the moral hold on their men given by one such exploit they were thereafter enabled to take the personal precautions which better befit the officer entrusted with the lives of others. The civilian at home poured scorn on the German officer " leading " his men from behind ; not so the fighting soldier, for he knew that when the occasion called, his officer enemy did not hesitate to risk, nay throw away his life, as an example. The story still lives of the German officer who led a forlorn hope mounted on a white horse.

The exploit, and the popular fame it brought, launched Scipio's military career so auspiciously as to earn him rapid advancement. For, less than two years later, 216 B.C., Livy's account speaks of him as one of the military tribunes, from whom the commanders of the legions were nominated, and in itself a post that made him one of the deputies or staff officers of the legion commander. If a parallel is desired, the nearest modern equivalent is a staff colonel.

This second glimpse of Scipio comes on the morrow of Cannæ, Rome's darkest hour, and it is curious that the future general, who, like Marlborough, was never to fight a battle that he did not win, should in his subordinate days have been witness of unrelieved disaster. There is no record of Scipio's share in the battle, but from Livy's account it seems clear that he was among the ten thousand survivors who escaped to the greater Roman camp across the River Aufidus, and further, one of the undaunted four thousand who, rather than surrender with their fellows, quitted the camp after nightfall, and eluding the Carthaginian horse, made their way to Canusium. Their situation was still perilous, for this place lay only some four miles distant, and why Hannibal did not follow up his success by the destruction of this remnant, isolated from succour, remains one of the enigmas of history, to all appearance a blemish on his generalship.

With the four thousand at Canusium were four military tribunes, and, as Livy tells us, " by the consent of all, the supreme command was vested in Publius Scipio, then a very young man, and Appius Claudius." Once more Scipio

shines amid the darkness of defeat; once more
a time of general disaster is the opportunity
of youth backed by character. Disruption, if
not mutiny, threatens. Word is brought that
men are saying that Rome is doomed, and that
certain of the younger patricians, headed by
Lucius Cæcilius Metellus, are proposing to leave
Rome to its fate and escape overseas to seek
service with some foreign king. These fresh
tidings of ill-fortune dismay and almost paralyse
the assembled leaders. But while the others
urge that a council be called to deliberate upon
the situation, Scipio acts. He declares " that it
is not a proper subject for deliberation ; that
courage and action, and not deliberation, were
necessary in such a calamity. That those who
desired the safety of the state would attend him
in arms forthwith ; that in no place was the
camp of the enemy more truly than where such
designs were meditated." Then, with only a
few companions, he goes straight to the lodging
of Metellus, surprising the plotters in council.
Drawing his sword, Scipio proclaims his purpose : " I swear that I will neither desert the
cause of Rome, nor allow any other citizen of
Rome to desert it. If knowingly I violate this
oath, may Jupiter visit with the most horrible
perdition my house, my family, and my fortune. I insist that you, Lucius Cæcilius, and

the rest of you present, take this oath ; and let the man who demurs be assured that this sword is drawn against him." The upshot is that, " terrified, as though they were beholding the victorious Hannibal, they all take the oath, and surrender themselves to Scipio to be kept in custody."

This danger quelled, Scipio and Appius, hearing that Varro, the surviving consul, had reached Venusia, sent a messenger there, placing themselves under his orders.

Scipio's next brief entry on the stage of history is in a different scene. His elder brother, Lucius, was a candidate for the ædileship,[1] and the younger Publius " for long did not venture to stand for the same office as his brother. But on the approach of the election, judging from the disposition of the people that his brother had a poor chance of being elected, and seeing that he himself was exceedingly popular, he came to the conclusion that the only means by which his brother would attain his object would be by their coming to an agreement and both of them making the attempt, and so he hit on the

---

[1] The ædileship was normally the first rung of the ladder to the higher magistracy. Its functions were those of a civic "Home Office"—the care of the city and the enforcement of the by-laws, the supervision of the markets and of prices and measures, the superintendence and organisation of the public games.

following plan. Seeing that his mother was
visiting the different temples and sacrificing to
the gods on behalf of his brother and generally
showing great concern about the result, he told
her, as a fact, that he had twice had the same
dream. He had dreamt that both he and his
brother had been elected to the ædileship, and
were going up from the Forum to their house
when she met them at the door and fell on
their necks and kissed them. She was affected
by this, as a woman would be, and exclaimed,
' Would I might see that day,' or something
similar. ' Then would you like us to try,
mother ? ' he said. Upon her consenting, as
she never dreamt he would venture on it, but
thought it was merely a casual joke—for he
was exceedingly young,—he begged her to get
a white toga ready for him at once, this being
the dress that candidates are in the habit of
wearing. What she had said had entirely gone
out of her head, and Scipio, waiting until he
received the white toga, appeared in the Forum
while his mother was still asleep. The people,
owing to the unexpectedness of the sight, and
owing to his previous popularity, received him
with enthusiastic surprise ; and afterwards, when
he went on to the station appointed for candidates and stood by his brother, they not only
conferred the office on Publius but on his brother

too for his sake, and both appeared at their home elected ædiles. When the news suddenly reached his mother's ears, she, overjoyed, met them at the door and embraced the young men with deep emotion, so that from this circumstance all who had heard of the dreams believed that Publius communed with the gods not only in his sleep, but still more in reality and by day."

"Now, it was not a matter of a dream at all; but as he was kind, munificent, and agreeable in his address, he reckoned on his popularity with the people, and so by cleverly adapting his action to the actual sentiment of the people and of his mother, he not only attained his object, but was believed to have acted under a sort of divine inspiration. For those who are incapable of taking an accurate view of opportunities, causes, and dispositions, attribute to the gods and to fortune the causes of what is accomplished by shrewdness and with calculation and foresight."

To some the deception, even though for a worthy end, may seem out of tune with the higher Roman virtues; and Livy, to whom as a Roman the artifice would appear less admirable than to Polybius, a Greek, leaves in doubt the origin of this habit of Scipio's, developed in his after career either by reason of its success or practice. Here is Livy's appreciation: "Scipio was undoubtedly the possessor of striking gifts; but besides that he had from childhood studied the art of their effective display. Whether there was some vein of superstition in his own temperament, or whether it was with the aim of securing for his commands the authority of inspired utterances, he rarely spoke in public without pretending to some nocturnal vision or supernatural suggestion." Livy may exaggerate the frequency, for he wrote at a later date, and legends grow round the characteristics of the great. Such supernatural claims only appear occasionally in Scipio's recorded utterances, and he, a supreme artist in handling human nature, would realise the value of reserving them for critical moments.

Livy continues: "In order to impress public opinion in this direction, he had made a practice from the day he reached manhood of never engaging in any business, public or private, without first paying a visit to the Capitol. There he would enter the sanctuary and pass some time, generally in solitude and seclusion. This habit . . . made converts to a belief, to which accident or design had given wide currency, that his origin was other than human. There was a story once widely believed about Alexander the Great, that his male parent had

B

been a huge serpent, often seen in his mother's chamber, but vanishing directly men appeared. This miracle was told again of Scipio . . . but he himself never cast ridicule upon it ; indeed, he rather lent it countenance by the course which he adopted of neither wholly disclaiming such tales nor openly asserting their truth." This last tale, incidentally, is repeated by several of the ancient writers and enshrined in ' Paradise Lost,' where Milton writes :—

> " He with Olympias, this with her that bore
> Scipio, the height of Rome."

The view that this claim to divine inspiration had a religious and not merely an intellectual basis gains some support from Scipio's conduct in the Syrian War of 190 B.C., when, because he was a member of the college of the priests of Mars, known as Salian priests, he stayed behind the army and indirectly kept it waiting at the Hellespont, as the rule bound him to stay where he was until the month ended.

Again, modern psychologists may suggest that his dreams were true and not invented, such is known to be the power of strong desire to fulfil itself in dreams. Whatever the explanation and the source of his " visions," there can be no doubt as to the skill with which he turned them to practical account. And it is a supreme moral tribute to Scipio that this power was exerted by him purely to further his country's good, never his own. When trouble and accusation came in later days, and an ungrateful State forgot its saviour, Scipio did not invoke any divine vision in his defence. That he so refrained is the more definite and the more significant, because, with other psychological means, he showed himself still the supreme "organist" of the human instrument.

Scipio's election to the ædileship is historically important, not only because it illumines the sources of his success and influence over men, but also for its light on the causes of his political decline, the self-imposed exile from an ungrateful country, which saw a marvellously brilliant career close in shadow. It is Livy who shows that his election was not so unopposed as Polybius's account would suggest; that the tribunes of the people opposed his pretensions to the office because he had not attained the legal age for candidature. Whereupon Scipio retorted that "if the citizens in general are desirous of appointing me ædile, I am old enough"—an appeal over the heads of the tribunes which was instantly successful, but which by its triumphant defiance of tradition and rule was likely to add resentment to the jealousy which inevitably accompanies the precocious success of youth.

CHAPTER II.

DAWN.

THESE three episodes form the prologue to the
real drama of Scipio's career. On this the curtain rises in 210 B.C., which, if not Rome's
blackest hour in her life and death struggle
with Carthage, was at least the greyest. That
conflict, which she had entered upon originally
in 264 B.C., was the inevitable sequel to the
supremacy of the Italian peninsula won by
her combination of political genius and military
vigour, for this supremacy could never be secure
so long as an alien sea power—Carthage—commanded the waters of the peninsula, a continual
menace to its seaboard and commerce. But
when, after many hazards, the close of the First
Punic War in 241 B.C. yielded Rome this mari-
time security, the vision and ambition of Hamilcar Barca not merely revived, but widened the
scope of the struggle between Rome and Carthage into one with world power or downfall

as the stakes. During the long interval of outward peace this Carthaginian Bismarck prepared the mental and material means for a stroke at the heart of the Roman power, educating his sons and followers to conceive the conquest of Rome as their goal, and using Spain as the training ground for the Barcine school of war, as well as the base of their forthcoming military effort. In 218 B.C., Hannibal, crossing the Alps, began his invasion of Italy to reap the harvest for which his father had sown the seeds. His victories on the Ticinus, the Trebia, at the Trasimene Lake, grew in scale until they reached their apex on the battlefield of Cannæ. If Roman fortitude, the loyalty of most of the Italian allies, and Hannibal's strategic caution then gained for Rome a reprieve, the passage of five years' unceasing warfare so drained her resources and exhausted her allies that by 211 B.C. Roman power, internally if not superficially, was perhaps nearer than ever before to a breakdown. A machine that is new and in good condition can withstand repeated severe shocks, but when badly worn a jar may suffice to cause its collapse. Such a jar came, for while Hannibal was campaigning in Southern Italy, destroying Roman armies if apparently drawing no nearer his object—the destruction of the Roman power,—the Carthaginian arms in Spain had been crowned with a victory that threatened Rome's footing on the peninsula.

For several years Scipio's father and uncle, Publius the elder and Gnæus, had been in command of the Roman forces there, winning repeated successes until, caught divided, the two brothers were defeated in turn, both falling on the battlefield. The shattered remnants of the Roman forces were driven north of the Ebro, and only a gallant rally by Marcius prevented the Romans being driven out of Spain. Even so their situation was precarious, for many of the Spanish tribes had forsaken the Romans in their hour of adversity. Though the determination of Rome itself, as before, was unbroken, and the disaster only spurred her to retrieve it, the choice of a successor proved difficult. Finally, it was decided to call an assembly of the people to elect a pro-consul for Spain. But no candidates offered themselves for the dangerous honour. " The people, at their wits' end, came down to the Campus Martius on the day of the election, where, turning towards the magistrate, they looked round at the countenances of their most eminent men, who were earnestly gazing at each other, and murmured bitterly that their affairs were in so ruinous a state, and the condition of the commonwealth so desperate, that no one dared under-

take the command in Spain. When suddenly
Publius Cornelius, son of Publius who had fallen
in Spain, who was about twenty-four years of
age, declared himself a candidate, and took his
station on an eminence by which he could be
seen by all " (Livy). His election was unanimous,
not only by every century, but by every man
there present. " But after the business had
been concluded, and the ardour and impetuosity
of their zeal had subsided, a sudden silence
ensued, and a secret reflection on what they
had done—whether their partiality had not got
the better of their judgment. They chiefly
regretted his youth ; but some were terrified
at the fortune which attended his house and
his name, for while the two families to which
he belonged were in mourning, he was going into
a province where he must carry on his operations amid the tombs of his father and his
uncle."

Realising the prevalence of these second
thoughts, these doubts, Scipio sought to offset
them by summoning an assembly, at which his
sagacious arguments did much to restore confidence. The secret of his sway, extraordinary
in one so young, over the crowd mind, especially
in times of crisis, was his profound self-confidence, which radiated an influence to which
the stories of his divine inspiration were but

auxiliary. Self-confidence is a term often used in a derogatory sense, but Scipio's was not only justified by results but essentially different, a spiritual exaltation which is epitomised by Aulus Gellius as " conscientia sui subnixus "—" lifted high on his consciousness of himself."

To the remains of the army in Spain ten thousand foot and a thousand horse were added, and taking these reinforcements, Scipio set sail with a fleet of thirty quinqueremes from the mouth of the Tiber. Coasting along the Gulf of Genoa, the Riviera shore, and the Gulf of Lions, he landed his troops just inside the Spanish frontier, and then marched overland to Tarraco—modern Tarragona. Here he received embassies from the various Spanish allies. His appreciation of the moral factor and of the value of personal observation, two vital elements in generalship, was shown in his earliest steps. The rival forces were in winter quarters, and before attempting to formulate any plan he visited the States of his allies and every one of the various parts of his army, seeking always by his attitude, even more than by his words, to rekindle confidence and dissipate the influence of past defeat. His own moral stature could not be better shown than by his treatment of Marcius, the man who had partly retrieved the Roman disasters, and thus

one whom an ambitious general might well
regard as a rival to his own position and fame.
But "Marcius he kept with him, and treated
him with such respect that it was perfectly
clear that there was nothing he feared less than
lest any one should stand in the way of his
own glory." Napoleon's jealousy of Moreau,
his deliberate overshadowing of his own mar-
shals, is in marked contrast with Scipio's attitude, and one of the finest of military tributes
to him is the abiding affection felt for him by
his subordinate generals. " No man is a hero
to his valet," and but few generals are heroes
to their chief staff officers, who see them inti-
mately in their nude qualities beneath the trappings of authority and public reputation. Loyal
subordinates will maintain the fiction of in-
fallibility for the good of the army, and so long
as is necessary, but they know the man as he
is, and in later years the truth leaks out. Thus
it is worth remembering that the verdict of
Polybius is founded on direct conversations with
Gaius Lælius, Scipio's coadjutor, and the one
man to whom he confided his military plans
before operations.

To the soldiers suffering under defeat he made
no reproaches, but aptly mingled an appeal to
their reason and to their spirit, reminding them
how often in Roman history early defeat had

been the presage to ultimate victory, how the
sure tilting of the balance had already begun,
the initial disasters found their counterpoise,
and in Italy and Sicily everything was going
prosperously. Then he pointed out that the
Carthaginian victories were not due to superior
courage, but " to the treachery of the Celtiberians and to rashness, the generals having been
cut off from each other owing to their trust in
the alliance of that people." Next he showed
how their disadvantages had shifted to the
other side, the Carthaginian armies " being encamped a long distance apart," their allies
estranged by tactlessness and tyranny, and,
above all, personal ill-feeling between the enemy's
commanders would make them slow to come
to each other's assistance. Finally, he kindled
their enthusiasm by touching their affection for
their lost leaders : " I will soon bring it to pass
that, as you can now trace in me a likeness to
my father and uncle in my features, countenance, and figure, I will so restore a copy of
their genius, honour, and courage, that every
man of you shall say that his commander,
Scipio, has either returned to life, or has been
born again."

His first step was to restore and fortify the
confidence of his own troops and allies, his next
to attack that of his enemies, to strike not at

their flesh but at their moral Achilles heel. His acute strategical insight, in a day when strategy, as distinct from battle tactics, had hardly been born, made him realise that Spain was the real key to the whole struggle. Spain was Hannibal's real base of operations; there he had trained his armies, and thence he looked for his reinforcements.

Scipio's first move was to apply his appreciation of the moral objective within the Spanish theatre of war. While others urged him to attack one of the Carthaginian armies, he decided to strike at their base, their life-line. First, he concentrated all his troops at one place, leaving one small but compact detachment of 3000 foot and 300 horse under Marcus Silanus to secure his own essential pivot of operations—Tarraco. Then, with all the rest, 25,000 foot and 2500 horse —here was true economy of force,—he crossed the Ebro, "revealing his plan to no one." " The fact was that he had decided not to do any of the things he had publicly announced, but to invest suddenly " New Carthage—modern Cartagena. To this end " he gave secret orders to Gaius Lælius, who commanded the fleet, who alone was aware of the project, to sail to that place, while he himself with his land forces marched rapidly against it." As Polybius sagely emphasises, calculation marked

this youth, for " he, in the first place, took in
hand a situation pronounced by most people as
desperate . . . and secondly, in dealing with it
he put aside the measures obvious to any one,
and planned out and decided on a course which
neither his enemies nor his friends expected."
" On his arrival in Spain he . . . inquired from
every one about the circumstances of the enemy,
and learnt that the Carthaginian forces were
divided into three bodies," Mago, near the pillars
of Hercules—Gibraltar ; Hasdrubal, son of Gisco,
near the mouth of the Tagus ; and Hasdrubal
Barca besieging a city in Central Spain not far
from modern Madrid.   None of them were
within less than ten days' march from New
Carthage ; he himself, as the event proved, was
within seven days' forced marches of it.   The
news of his attack must take several days to
reach them, and if he could take it by a surprise
coup de main he would forestall any aid, and
" in the event of failure he could, since he was
master of the sea, place his troops in a position
of safety."   Polybius further tells us how " during the winter he made detailed inquiries from
people acquainted with it."   " He learnt that
it stood almost alone among Spanish cities in
possessing harbours fit for a fleet and for naval
forces, and also that it was for the Carthaginians
the direct sea crossing from Africa.   Next he

heard that the Carthaginians kept the bulk of their money and their war material in this city, as well as their hostages from the whole of Spain ; and, what was of most importance, that the trained soldiers who garrisoned the citadel were only about a thousand strong, because no one dreamt that while the Carthaginians were masters of nearly the whole of Spain it would enter any one's head to besiege the city, while the remaining population was exceedingly large, but composed of artisans, tradesmen, and sailors, men very far from having any military experience. This he considered to be a thing that would tell against the city if he appeared suddenly before it "—the moral calculation again. " Abandoning, therefore, all other projects, he spent his time while in winter quarters in preparing for this," but " he concealed the plan from every one except Gaius Lælius." The account shows that he was master of two more attributes of generalship—the power to keep his intentions secret until their disclosure was necessary for the execution of the plan, and the wisdom to realise that military success depends largely on the thoroughness of the previous preparation.

Polybius's assertion that Scipio's move was due to masterly calculation, and not to inspiration or fortune, is confirmed indirectly by the reference to a letter of Scipio's which he had seen, and directly by Livy's quotation of Scipio's speech to the troops before the attack. One phrase epitomises the strategic idea: " You will in actuality attack the walls of a single city, but in that single city you will have made yourselves masters of all Spain," and he explains exactly how capture of the hostages, the treasure, and the war stores will be turned to their advantage and react to the enemy's disadvantage, moral, economic, and material. Even if Livy's phrase was coined to meet Scipio's fact, its note is so exactly in accord with Scipio's actions as to give it a ring of basic truth.

CHAPTER III.

THE STORM OF CARTAGENA.

ON the seventh day from the start of the march
Scipio arrived before the city and encamped,
the fleet arriving simultaneously in the harbour,
thus cutting off communication on all sides.
This harbour formed a circular bottle, its mouth
almost corked by an island, while Cartagena
itself was like a candle stuck in the bottom of
the bottle, the city standing on a narrow rocky
spit of land protruding from the mainland. This
small peninsula bore a distinct resemblance to
Gibraltar, and the isthmus joining it to the
mainland was only some four hundred yards
across. The city was guarded on two sides by
the sea, and on the west by a lagoon. Here
was a hard nut to crack, seemingly impregnable
to any action save a blockade, and this, time
prevented.

Scipio's first step was to ensure his tactical
security by defending the outer side of his camp
with a palisade and double trench stretching

from sea to sea. On the inner side, facing the
isthmus, he erected no defences, partly because
the nature of the ground gave protection, and
partly in order not to hinder the free movement
of his assaulting troops. The Carthaginian commander, Mago, to oppose him armed two thousand of the sturdiest citizens, and posted them
by the landward gate for a sortie. The rest he
distributed to defend the walls to the best of
their power, while of his own regulars he disposed five hundred in the citadel on the top of
the peninsula, and five hundred on the eastern
hill.

Next day Scipio encircled the city with ships,
throwing a constant stream of missiles, and about
the third hour [1] sent forward along the isthmus
two thousand picked men with the ladder-bearers,
for its narrowness prevented a stronger force
being deployed. Appreciating the handicap of
their cramped position if counter-attacked by
the yet unshaken defenders, he astutely designed
to turn this handicap to his own advantage.
The expected sortie came as soon as Scipio
sounded the bugle for assault, and a close-
matched struggle ensued. " But as the assistance sent to either side was not equal, the Carthaginians arriving through a single gate and
from a longer distance, the Romans from close

---

[1] The Roman day began at sunrise.

by and from several points, the battle for this reason was an unequal one. For Scipio had purposely posted his men close to the camp itself in order to entice the enemy as far out as possible " (Livy says the Roman advanced troops retired according to orders on the reserves), " well knowing that if he destroyed those who were, so to speak, the steel edge of the population he would cause universal dejection, and none of those inside would venture out of the gate again " (Polybius). This last point was essential for the freedom of his decisive move.

By the skilful infusion of successive reserves into the combat, the Carthaginian onset was first stemmed and then driven back in disorder, the pursuit being pressed so promptly that the Romans nearly succeeded in forcing an entrance on the heels of the fugitives. Even as it was, the scaling ladders were able to be put up in full security, but the great height of the walls hampered the escaladers, and the assault was beaten off. Polybius gives a picture of the Roman commander during this phase which reveals how he combined personal influence and control with the duty of avoiding rash exposure : " Scipio took part in the battle, but studied his safety as far as possible, for he had with him three men carrying large shields, who, holding these

c

close, covered the surface exposed to the wall, and so afforded him protection." " . . . Thus he could both see what was going on, and being seen by all his men he inspired the combatants with great spirit. The consequence was that nothing was omitted which was necessary in the engagement, but the moment that circumstances suggested any step to him, he set to work at once to do what was necessary."

In modern war no feature has told more heavily against decisive results than the absence of the commander's personal observation and control. Scipio's method, viewed in the light of modern science, may suggest a way to revive this influence. Peradventure the commander of the future will go aloft in an aeroplane, protected by a patrol of fighters, and in communication by wireless telephony with his staff.

Scipio had achieved his first object of wearing down the defenders, and checking the likelihood of further interference with his plans from Carthaginian sorties. The way was thus paved for his next decisive move. To develop this he was only waiting for the ebb of the tide, and this design had been conceived by him long since at Tarraco, where, from inquiries among fishermen who knew Cartagena, he had learnt that at low water the lagoon was fordable.

For this project he assembled five hundred

men with ladders on the shore of the lagoon,
and meanwhile reinforced his forces in the isthmus
with both men and ladders, enough to ensure
that in the next direct assault " the whole extent
of the walls should be covered with escaladers "
—an early example of the modern tactical axiom
that a " fixing " attack should be on the broadest
possible front in order to occupy the enemy's
attention and prevent him turning to meet
the decisive blow elsewhere.   He launched this
assault simultaneously with a landing attack by
the fleet, and when it was at its height " the
tide began to ebb and the water gradually re-
ceded from the edge of the lagoon, a strong and
deep current setting in through the channel to
the neighbourhood, so that to those who were
not prepared for the sight the thing appeared
incredible.   But Scipio had his guides ready,
and bade all the men told off for this service
enter the water and have no fear.   He, indeed,
possessed a particular talent for inspiring confidence and sympathy in his troops when he
called upon them.   Now when they obeyed and
raced through the shallow water, it struck the
whole army that it was the work of some god
. . . and their courage was redoubled " (Polybius).   Of this episode Livy says : " Scipio,
crediting this discovery, due to his own diligence
and penetration, to the gods and to miracle,

which had turned the course of the sea, withdrawn it from the lake, and opened ways never
before trodden by human feet to afford a passage
to the Romans, ordered them to follow Neptune
as their guide." But it is interesting to see that,
while exploiting the moral effect of this idea,
he made practical use of less divine guides. The
five hundred passed without difficulty through
the lagoon, reached the wall, and mounted it
without opposition, because all the defenders
" were engaged in bringing succour to that
quarter in which the danger appeared." " The
Romans having once taken the wall, at first
marched along it, sweeping the enemy off it."
They were clearly imbued with the principle
that a penetration must be promptly widened
before it is deepened—a principle which in the
war of 1914-1918 was only learnt after hard
lessons, at Loos and elsewhere. Next they con-
verged on the landward gate, already assailed
in front, and taking the defenders in rear and
by surprise, overpowered the resistance and
opened the way for the main body of the attackers. The walls thus captured, Scipio at once
exploited his success. For while the mass of
those who had by now scaled the walls set about
the customary massacre of the townsmen, Scipio
himself took care to keep in regular formation
those who entered by the gate, and led them

against the citadel. Here Mago, once he " saw that the city had undoubtedly been captured," surrendered.

If the massacre of the townspeople is revolting to modern ideas, it was the normal custom then and for many centuries thereafter, and with the Romans was a deliberate policy aimed at the moral factor rather than mere insensate slaughter. The direct blow at the civil population, who are the seat of the hostile will, may indeed be revived by the potentialities of aircraft, which can jump, halmawise, over the armed " men " who form the shield of the enemy nation. Such a course, if militarily practicable, is the logical one, and ruthless logic usually overcomes the humaner sentiments in a life and death struggle.

Proof of the discipline of Scipio's troops is that the massacre ceased on a signal after the citadel surrendered, and only then did the troops begin pillaging. The massacre, however difficult for modern minds to excuse, was a military measure, and the conduct of the action was not impeded by the individual's desire to obtain loot or " souvenirs "—an undisciplined impulse which has affected even recent battles.

The massacre, moreover, was partly offset by Scipio's generous, if diplomatic, conduct to the vanquished, once the initial ruthlessness had

achieved its purpose of quenching the citizens'
will to resist. Of the ten thousand male prisoners,
he set free all who were citizens of New Carthage,
and restored their property. The artisans, to
the number of two thousand, he declared the
property of Rome, but promised them their
freedom when the war was over if they "showed
goodwill and industry in their several crafts."
The pick of the remainder were taken for sea
service, thus enabling him to man the captured
vessels and so increase the size of his fleet ; these
also were promised their freedom after the final
defeat of Carthage. Even to Mago and the
other Carthaginian leaders he acted as became
a chivalrous victor, ordering Lælius to pay them
due attention, until subsequently they were sent
to Rome in the latter's charge, as a tangible
evidence of victory which would revive the
Romans' spirits, and lead them to redouble their
efforts to support him. Finally, he won new
allies for himself by his kindness to the Spanish
hostages, for instead of retaining them in his
custody as unwilling guarantees, he sent them
home to their own States.

Two incidents, related by both Livy and
Polybius, throw Scipio's character into relief,
and enhance his reputation as one of the most
humane and far-sighted of the great conquerors.
"When one of the captive women, the wife of

Mandonius, who was brother to Andobales, King of the Ilergetes, fell at his feet and entreated him with tears to treat them with more proper consideration than the Carthaginians had done, he was touched, and asked her what they stood in need of. . . . Upon her making no reply, he sent for the officials appointed to attend on the women. When they presented themselves, and assured him that they kept the women generously supplied with all they required, she repeated her entreaty, upon which Scipio was still more puzzled, and conceiving the idea that the officials were neglecting their duty and had now made a false statement, he bade the woman be of good cheer, saying that he would himself appoint other attendants, who would see to it that they were in want of nothing. The old lady, after some hesitation, said, 'General, you do not take me rightly if you think that our present petition is about our food.' Scipio then understood what she meant, and noticing the youth and beauty of the daughters of Andobales and the other princes, he was forced to tears, recognising in how few words she had pointed out to him the danger to which they were exposed. So now he made it clear to her that he understood, and grasping her hand bade her and the rest be of good cheer, for he would look after them as if they were his own sisters and children, and would appoint trustworthy men to attend on them " (Polybius).

The second incident, as told by Polybius, was : " Some young Romans came across a girl of surpassing bloom and beauty, and being aware that Scipio was fond of women brought her to him . . . saying that they wished to make a present of the damsel to him. He was overcome and astonished by her beauty, and he told them that had he been in a private position no present would have been more welcome, but as he was the general it would be the least welcome of any. . . . So he expressed his gratitude to the young men, but called the girl's father, and handing her over to him, at once bade him give her in marriage to whomever of the citizens he preferred. The self-restraint and moderation Scipio showed on this occasion secured him the warm approbation of his troops." Livy's account enlarges the picture, saying that she was previously betrothed to a young chief of the Celtiberians, named Allucius, who was desperately enamoured of her ; that Scipio, hearing this, sent for Allucius and presented her to him ; and that when his parents pressed thank-offerings upon him, he gave these to Allucius as a dowry from himself. This kindly and tactful act not only spread his praises through the Spanish tribes, but earned a more tangible reinforcement, for Allucius reappeared a few days later with fourteen hundred horsemen to join Scipio.

With his own troops also his blend of generosity and wisdom was no less noticeable. The booty was scrupulously divided according to the Roman custom, which ensured that all was pooled ; and as he had so cleverly used every art to inspire them beforehand, so now he appreciated the moral value of praise and distinctive reward for feats achieved. Better still was his haste to make the victory secure against any unforeseen slip or enemy counter-stroke. He had led back the legions to their entrenched camp on the same day as the city's capture, leaving Lælius with the marines to guard the city. Then, after one day's rest, he began a course of military exercises to keep the troops up to concert pitch. On the first day the soldiers had to double three and a half miles in their armour, and the legions carried out various drill movements ; the second day they had to polish up, repair, and examine their arms ; the third day they rested ; and the fourth day they carried out weapon training, "some of them sword-fighting with wooden swords covered with leather and with a button on the point, while others practised javelin throwing, the javelins also having a button on the point " ; on the fifth day they began the course again, and continued during their stay at Cartagena. "The rowers and marines, pushing out to sea when the weather was calm, made trial of the manœuvring of their ships in mock sea-fights." "The general went round to all the works with equal attention. At one time he was employed in the dockyard with his fleet, at another he exercised with the legions; sometimes he would devote himself to the inspection of the works, which every day were carried out with the greatest eagerness by a multitude of artificers, both in the workshops and in the armoury and docks" (Livy).

Then, when the walls had been repaired, he left adequate detachments to hold the city, and set out for Tarraco with the army and the fleet.

In summing up this first brilliant exploit in command, the first tribute is due to the strategic vision and judgment shown in the choice of Cartagena as his objective. Those who exalt the main armed forces of the enemy as the primary objective are apt to lose sight of the fact that the destruction of these is only a means to the end, which is the subjugation of the hostile will. In many cases this means is essential—the only safe one, in fact; but in other cases the opportunity for a direct and secure blow at the enemy's base may offer itself, and of its possibility and value this master-stroke of

Scipio's is an example, which deserves the reflection of modern students of war.

In the sphere of tactics there is a lesson in his consummate blending of the principles of surprise and security, first in the way he secured every offensive move from possible interference or mischance, second in the way he " fixed " the enemy before, and during, his decisive manœuvre. To strike at an enemy who preserves his freedom of action is to risk hitting the air and being caught off one's balance. It is to gamble on chances, and the least mischance is liable to upset the whole plan. Yet how often in war, and even in peace-time manœuvres, have commanders initiated some superficially brilliant manœuvre only to find that the enemy have slipped away from the would-be knockout, because the assailant forgot the need of " fixing." And the tactical formula of *fixing plus decisive manœuvre* is, after all, but the domestic proverb, " First catch your hare, then cook it." Precept, however, is simpler than practice, and not least of Scipio's merits is his superb calculation of the time factor in his execution of the formula.

CHAPTER IV.

THE BATTLE OF BÆCULA.

WITH Cartagena in his grip, Scipio had gained the strategical initiative, which is by no means identical with the offensive. To attack the Carthaginian field armies while he was still markedly inferior in numbers would be to throw away this advantage and imperil all that he had gained. On the other hand, he held the key to any possible Carthaginian move. If they moved to regain Cartagena, itself impregnable if adequately garrisoned, and still more so when the defender had command of the sea, he lay on their flank with his main striking force. If they moved against him, he would have the advantage of choosing his own ground, and, in addition, Cartagena would threaten their rear, for his command of the sea would enable him to transfer forces there. If they remained passive, and this inaction proved their choice, they would suffer the handicap due to the loss of their base, depot, and main line of communica-

tion with Carthage. Nothing could have suited
Scipio better, for the respite allowed the moral
effect of Cartagena's capture to sink into the
minds of the Spanish, and allowed him also
time to win over fresh allies to offset his numerical
handicap. The result proved the soundness of
his calculations, for during the next winter
Edeco, Andobales, and Mandonius, three of the
most powerful chieftains in Spain, came over
to him, and most of the Iberian tribes followed
their example. As Polybius justly says, "Those
who have won victories are far more numerous
than those who have used them to advantage,"
and Scipio, more than any other great captain,
seems to have grasped the truth that the fruits
of victory lie in the after years of peace—a truth
hardly realised even to-day, despite the lessons
of Versailles.

The outcome was that Hasdrubal Barca, faced
with this shifting of the balance, felt forced to
take the offensive. This gage Scipio, thus reinforced, was not loth to accept, for it promised
him the chance to deal with one hostile army
before the others had joined it. But with the
principle of security impressed on his mind, he
still further strengthened his forces, to meet the
possibility that he might be forced to fight more
than one army at once. This he did by the
ingenious measure of hauling his ships on shore

at Tarraco and adding their crews to his army, a course which was feasible because the Carthaginian ships had been swept from the sea, and because he was about to advance into the interior. His foresight in exploiting the workshop resources of Cartagena gave him an ample reserve of weapons from which to arm them.

While Hasdrubal was still preparing, Scipio moved. On his advance from his winter quarters he was joined by Andobales and Mandonius with their forces, handing over to them their daughters, whom he had apparently retained—because of their key importance,—unlike the other hostages taken at Cartagena. Next day he made a treaty with them, of which the essential part was that they should follow the Roman commanders and obey their orders. Scipio evidently appreciated the importance of unity of command. The army of Hasdrubal lay in the district of Castalon, near the town of Bæcula on the upper reaches of the Bætis, to-day called the Guadalquiver. On the approach of the Romans he shifted his camp to an admirable defensive position—a small but high plateau, deep enough for security, and wide enough to deploy his troops, difficult of access on the flanks, and with a river protecting its rear. The formation of this plateau, moreover, was in two " steps," and on the lower Hasdrubal

BAECULA
(Bailen)

HARINA

TAROSA

HASDRUBAL'S
CAMP

RIO GUADIEL

SCIPIO

LIGHT TROOPS

LAELIUS

SCIPIO'S
CAMP

BATTLE OF BAECULA

BRITISH MILES

0   ½   1

□ □ □   CARTHAGINIAN
■ ■ ■   ROMAN   } LIGHT TROOPS

▭   CARTHAGINIAN
▬   ROMAN   } MAIN BODY

SITE BASED ON KROMAYER-VEITH.

posted his screen of light troops, Numidian horse and Balearic slingers, while on the higher ridge behind he entrenched his camp.

Scipio for a moment was at a loss how to tackle such a strong position, but not daring to wait lest the two other Carthaginian armies should come up, he devised a plan. He sent the velites and other light troops to scale the first " step " of the enemy's position, and despite the rocky ascent and the shower of darts and stones, their determination and practice in using cover enabled them to gain the crest. Once a footing was secured, their better weapons and training for close combat prevailed over skirmishers trained for missile action with ample space for a running fight. Thus the Carthaginian light troops were driven back in disorder on the higher ridge.

Scipio, who had the rest of his army ready but inside their camp, " now despatched the whole of his light troops with orders to support the frontal attack," while, dividing his heavy foot into two bodies, he himself led one half round the left flank of the enemy's position, and sent Lælius with the other to skirt the opposite flank of the ridge until he could find a good line of ascent. Making the shorter circuit, Scipio's men climbed the ridge first, and fell on the Car- thaginians' flank before they had properly de-

ployed, as Hasdrubal, relying on the strength
of his position, had delayed leading his main
forces out of the camp. Thus trapped before
they had formed up and while still on the move,
the Carthaginians were thrown into disorder,
and during the confusion Lælius came up and
charged their other flank. It may be mentioned
that Livy, in contradiction to Polybius, says
that Scipio led the left wing and Lælius the
right, a divergence obviously due to whether the
position is considered from the attackers' or the
defenders' side.

Polybius states that Hasdrubal's original intention in case of a reverse had been to retreat
to Gaul, and after recruiting as many of the
natives as possible, to join his brother Hannibal
in Italy. Whether this be surmise or fact, as
soon as Hasdrubal realised the battle was lost
he hurried from the hill with his treasure and
his elephants, and collecting in his retreat as
many of the fugitives as he could, retired up
the river Tagus in the direction of the Pyrenees.
But Scipio's double envelopment, and still more
his foresight in sending beforehand two cohorts
to block two of the main lines of retreat, caught
as in a net the bulk of the Carthaginian troops.
Eight thousand were slain, twelve thousand
taken prisoners. While the African prisoners
were sold as slaves, Scipio once more showed

his political sagacity by sending home the Spanish prisoners without ransom.

Polybius says, " Scipio did not think it advisable to follow Hasdrubal, as he was afraid of being attacked by the other generals," and to a military critic the reason is convincing. It would have been foolhardy to press farther into the mountainous interior with twc more hostile armies, superior in strength, able to converge on him or to cut him off from his base. A bare statement of the military problem is ample answer to those, mainly civil historians, who decry Scipio on the score that he allowed Hasdrubal to quit Spain and move into Italy on his ill-fated attempt to join Hannibal. It is interesting to note that Hasdrubal followed the route of Wellington after Vittoria, making his way to the northern coast of Spain, and crossing by modern San Sebastian and the western gap where the Pyrenees slope down to the sea.

To pretend that Scipio, had he remained on the defensive, could have barred this passage is absurd, based as he was on the eastern coast. Either of the other Carthaginian armies could have contained him while Hasdrubal slipped through one of the numerous western passes, or again, if he attempted so distant a move through wild and mountainous country, not only would he have exposed his base but have

D

invited disaster. But for Scipio's offensive and victory at Bæcula, Hasdrubal could have entered Gaul in force, and thus have avoided the two years' delay—so fatal to the Carthaginian cause —enforced by his need to recruit and reorganise his army in Gaul before passing on.

The aftermath of Bæcula, like that of Cartagena, contains two incidents which illumine Scipio's character. The first was when the Spanish allies, old and new, all saluted him as king. Edeco and Andobales had done so when joining him on the outward march, and he had then paid little attention, but when the title was re-echoed so universally he took action. Summoning them to an assembly, he " told them that he wished to be called kingly by them and actually to be kingly, but that he did not wish to be king or to be called so by any one. After saying this he ordered them to call him general " (Polybius). Livy, relating this incident in other words, adds, " Even barbarians were sensible of the greatness of mind which from such an elevation could despise a name, at the greatness of which the rest of mankind was overawed." It is assuredly the clearest indication of Scipio's mental stature that in the first flush of triumph this youthful conqueror could preserve such self-command and balance of mind. Weighed solely by his character, apart from his achievements, Scipio has claims to be considered the highest embodiment of the Roman virtues, humanised and broadened by the culture of Greece, yet proof against its degenerate tendencies.

The second incident, whether it be due solely to the sympathetic insight which peculiarly distinguished him or to the diplomatic foresight which made this gift of such inestimable value to his country, is equally significant. The quæstor selling the African prisoners came upon a handsome boy, and learning that he was of royal blood, sent him to Scipio. In answer to the latter's questions, the boy said that he was a Numidian, his name Massiva, and that he had come to Spain with his uncle Masinissa, who had raised a force of cavalry to assist the Carthaginians. That, disobeying his uncle, who considered him too young to be in battle, "he had clandestinely taken a horse and arms, and, without his uncle's knowledge, gone on the field, where, his horse falling, he was thrown and taken prisoner." Scipio asked him whether he wished to return to Masinissa, and on his assenting with tears of joy, presented the youth with "a gold ring, a vest with broad purple border, a Spanish cloak with gold clasp, and a horse completely caparisoned, and then released him, ordering a party of horse to escort him as far as he chose."

Scipio then fell back on his base, and spent the remainder of the summer in exploiting the effect of the victory by securing the alliance of most of the Spanish States. His wisdom in not following up Hasdrubal was justified by the fact that within a few days after the battle of Bæcula, Hasdrubal, son of Gisco, and Mago arrived to join Hasdrubal Barca. This arrival, too late to save the last-named from defeat, served to bring about a conference to settle their future plans. Realising that Scipio by his diplomacy and his victories had gained the sympathies of almost all Spain, they decided that Mago should transfer his forces to Hasdrubal Barca, and go to the Balearic Isles to raise fresh auxiliaries ; that Hasdrubal Barca should move into Gaul as soon as possible before his remaining Spanish troops deserted, and then march on into Italy ; that Hasdrubal, son of Gisco, should retire into the remotest part of Lusitania, near Gades—modern Cadiz,—where alone the Carthaginians might hope for Spanish aid. Finally, Masinissa, with a body of three thousand horse, was to have a roving commission, his object being to harass and ravage the lands of the Romans and of their Spanish allies.

The chronology of these years is somewhat difficult to determine, but the victory at Bæcula

seems to have been in 208 B.C. The next year
Scipio's hold on the country was threatened
afresh. A new general, Hanno, had come with
a fresh army from Carthage to replace Hasdrubal
Barca. Mago also had returned from the Balearic
Isles, and after arming native levies in Celti-
beria, which embraced parts of modern Arragon
and Old Castile, was joined by Hanno. Nor
was the threat only from one direction, for
Hasdrubal, son of Gisco, had advanced from
Gades into Bætica (Andalusia). If Scipio moved
into the interior against Hanno and Mago he
might find Hasdrubal across his rear. Therefore
he detached his lieutenant, Silanus, with ten
thousand foot and five hundred horse, to attack
the former, while he himself apparently kept
watch and check on Hasdrubal.

Silanus marched so fast, despite the rugged
defiles and thick woods on his route, that he
came on the Carthaginians before any messengers
or even rumours had warned them of his approach. The advantage of surprise offset his
inferior strength, and falling first on the Celtiberian camp, where no proper watch or guard
was kept, he had routed them before the Carthaginians had come up to their aid. Mago
with almost all the cavalry and two thousand
foot fled from the field as soon as the verdict

was clear, and retreated towards the province
of Gades. But Hanno and those of the Carthaginians who arrived on the field when the
battle was decided were taken prisoners, and
the Celtiberian levies so thoroughly dispersed
as to nip in the bud the danger that other
tribes might copy their example and join the
Carthaginians.

It is characteristic of Scipio that he was un-
stinting in his praise of Silanus. Having thus
ensured the security of his flank for an advance
southward, he moved against Hasdrubal, whereupon the latter not only fell back in indecent
haste, but lest his united army should attract
Scipio on to him, he broke it up to form small
garrisons for the various walled towns.

Scipio, seeing the enemy thus abandon himself to a passive defensive, decided that there
was no object in conducting a series of petty
sieges likely to drain his own force without
adequate advantage. However, he sent his
brother Lucius to storm one town, Orinx, which
served Hasdrubal as a strategical pivot from
which to make incursions into the inland States.
This task Lucius carried out successfully, and
Scipio's nature is again instanced in the record
that he commended Lucius with the highest
praise, representing the capture of Orinx as

equal in importance to his own feat at Cartagena. As winter was by now approaching he
dismissed the legions to winter quarters, and
sent his brother with Hanno and other distinguished prisoners to Rome.

CHAPTER V.

THE BATTLE OF ILIPA.

In the spring of 206 B.C. the Carthaginians made
their last great effort. Hasdrubal, encouraged
by Mago, Hannibal's brother, raised and armed
fresh levies, and with an army of seventy thousand foot, four thousand horse, and thirty-two
elephants moved north to Ilipa (or Silpia), which
was not far from where Seville stands to-day.
Scipio advanced south from Tarraco to meet the
Carthaginians, collecting auxiliaries at Bæcula
on his way. When he drew near the Bætis and
got fuller information of the opposing force, he
appreciated the formidable nature of the problem.
He felt convinced that with the Roman legions
only he would not be a match for so large an
enemy army, yet to use a large proportion of
allies and rely on their support was to risk the
fate of his father and uncle, whose downfall was
due to the sudden desertion of their allies.
Therefore he decided to use them for the purpose
of impressing and misleading the enemy " by

an imposing show," but leave the main fighting rôle to his own legions. He had learnt, like Wellington two thousand years later, that it was wiser not to place reliance on the co-operation of his Spanish allies. The French in Morocco have imbibed it afresh. Advancing towards Ilipa with a total force, Romans and allies, of forty-five thousand foot and three thousand horse, he came in sight of the Carthaginians, and encamped on certain low hills opposite them. It deserves notice that his advance was on a line which, in the event of victory, would cut them off from the nearest road to Gades, this road running along the south bank of the Bætis river.

Mago, thinking this a favourable chance for a sudden disorganising blow, took most of his cavalry as well as Masinissa with his Numidian horse, and attacked those engaged in forming the camp. But Scipio, as usual, imbued with the principle of security, had foreseen such a possibility, and had posted his own cavalry ready in concealment under shelter of a hill. These charged the forward part of the Carthaginian horse in flank and threw them into disorder, and though the rear echelons, coming up to reinforce the attack, restored the balance for a time, the issue was settled by the sortie of a large body of legionaries from the Roman

camp. At first the Carthaginians fell back in
good order ; but as the pursuit was vigorously
pressed, they broke up and fled to the shelter
of their own camp. The result gave Scipio an
initial moral advantage.

The two camps lay facing each other across
a valley between the two low ridges. For several
successive days Hasdrubal led his army out and
offered battle. On each occasion Scipio waited
until the Carthaginians were moving out before
he followed suit. Neither side, however, began
the attack, and towards sundown the two armies,
weary of standing, retired to their camps—the
Carthaginians always first. One cannot doubt,
in view of the upshot, that on Scipio's side the
delay had a special motive. On each occasion
also the legions were placed in the Roman centre
opposite to the Carthaginian and African regulars, with the Spanish allies on the wings of
each army. It became common talk in the
camps that this order of battle was definite, and
Scipio waited until this belief had taken firm
hold.

Then he acted. He had observed that the
Carthaginians made their daily advance at a late
hour, and had himself purposely waited still
later, to fix this habit on his opponent's mind.
Late in the evening he sent orders through the
camp that the troops should be fed and armed

before daylight, and the cavalry have their horses saddled. Then, while it was scarcely yet daylight, he sent on the cavalry and light troops to attack the enemy's outposts, and himself followed with the legions. This was the first surprise change, and its effect was that the Carthaginians, caught napping by the onset of the Roman cavalry and light troops, had to arm themselves and sally forth without a meal. It further ensured that Hasdrubal would have no time to alter his normal dispositions, even should the idea occur to him. For the second surprise change was that Scipio reversed his former order of battle, and placed the Spanish in his centre and the legions on the wings.

The Roman infantry made no attempt to advance for some hours, the reason for this being Scipio's desire and design to let his hungry opponents feel the effects of their lost breakfast. There was no risk to his other surprise change by so doing, for once drawn up in order of battle the Carthaginians dared not alter their array in face of a watchful and ready opponent. The skirmishing fight between the opposing cavalry and light troops remained indecisive, each when hard-pressed able to take shelter behind their own infantry. Eventually, when Scipio judged the time ripe, he sounded a retreat, and received his skirmishers back through the intervals between the cohorts, then placing them in reserve behind each wing, the velites behind the heavy infantry and the cavalry behind the velites.

It was about the seventh hour[1] when he ordered the line to advance, but the Spanish centre only at a slow pace. On arriving within eight hundred yards of the enemy, Scipio, with the right wing, turned to the right and, wheeling left, mad: an oblique advance outwards by successive cohorts—in column. He had previously sent a messenger to Silanus and Marcius, commanding the left wing, to manœuvre similarly. Advancing rapidly, so that the slow moving centre was well *refused*, the Roman infantry cohorts wheeled successively inwards into line as they neared the enemy, and fell directly on the enemy's flanks, which but for this manœuvre would have overlapped them. While the heavy infantry thus pressed the enemy's wings in front, the cavalry and the velites, under orders, wheeled outwards, and sweeping round the enemy's flanks took them in enfilade. This convergent blow on each wing, sufficiently disruptive because it forced the defenders to face attack from two directions simultaneously, was made more decisive in that it fell on the Spanish irregulars. To add to Hasdrubal's troubles the cavalry flank attacks

_____
[1] The Roman day began at sunrise.

BATTLE of ILIPA
SCIPIO'S MANOEUVRE.

HASDRUBAL'S CAMP

CAVALRY

CAVALRY

SPANISH

AFRICANS

SPANISH

ROMAN FOOT

" VELITES

" CAVALRY

SCIPIO'S SPANISH
ALLIES

CARTHAGINIAN
ELEPHANTS

SCIPIO'S
CAMP

drove his elephants, mad with fright, in upon the Carthaginian centre, spreading confusion.

All this time the Carthaginian centre was standing helplessly inactive, unable to help the wings for fear of attack by Scipio's Spaniards, who threatened it without coming to close quarters. Scipio's calculation had enabled him to " fix " the enemy's centre with a minimum expenditure of force, and thus to effect the maximum concentration for his decisive double manœuvre.

Hasdrubal's wings destroyed, the centre, worn out by hunger and fatigue, fell back, at first in good order, but gradually under relentless pressure they broke up, fleeing to their entrenched camp. A drenching downpour, churning the ground in mud under the soldiers' feet, gave them a temporary respite, and prevented the Romans storming the camp on their heels. During the night Hasdrubal evacuated his camp, but as Scipio's strategic advance had placed the Romans across the line of retreat to Gades, he was forced to retire down the western bank towards the Atlantic. Nearly all his Spanish Allies deserted him.

Scipio's light troops were evidently alive to the duty of maintaining contact with the enemy, for he got word from them as soon as it was light of Hasdrubal's departure. He at once followed them up, sending the cavalry ahead, and so rapid was the pursuit that, despite being misled by guides in attempting a short cut to get across Hasdrubal's new line of retreat, the cavalry and velites caught him up. Harassing him continuously, by attacks in flank or in rear, they forced such frequent halts that the legions were able to come up. "After this it was no longer a fight, but a butchering as of cattle," till only Hasdrubal and six thousand half-armed men escaped to the neighbouring hills, out of seventy odd thousand who had fought at Ilipa. The Carthaginians hastily fortified a camp on the highest summit, but though its inaccessibility hindered assault, lack of food caused a constant stream of deserters. At last Hasdrubal left his troops by night, and reaching the sea, not far distant, took ship to Gades, and Mago soon followed him.

Scipio thereupon left Silanus with a force to await the inevitable surrender of the camp, and returned to Tarraco.

Military history contains no more classic example of generalship than this battle of Ilipa. Rarely has so complete a victory been gained by a weaker over a stronger force, and this result was due to a perfect application of the principles of *surprise* and *concentration*, that is in essence an example for all time. How crude does

Frederick's famed oblique order appear beside
Scipio's double oblique manœuvre and envelopment, which effected a crushing concentration
du fort au faible while the enemy's centre was
surely fixed.   Scipio left the enemy no chance for
the change of front which cost Frederick so dear
at Kolin.   Masterly as were his battle tactics, still
more remarkable perhaps were the decisiveness
and rapidity of their exploitation, which found
no parallel in military history until Napoleon
came to develop the pursuit as the vital com-
plement of battle, and one of the supreme tests
of generalship.   To Scipio no cavalry leader
could have complained as Maharbal, whether
justly or not, to Hannibal, " You know, indeed,
how to win a victory, Hannibal, but you know
not how to use one ! "

But Scipio, in whom the idea of strategic exploitation was as inborn as the tactical, was not
content to rest on his laurels.   Already he was
looking to the future, directing his view on
Africa.   As he had seen that Cartagena was the
key to Spain, that Spain was the key to the
situation in Italy, so he saw that Africa was
the key to the whole struggle.   Strike at Africa,
and he would not only relieve Italy of Hannibal's
ever-menacing presence—a menace which he had
already reduced by paralysing Hannibal's source
of reinforcement, — but would undermine the

foundations of Carthaginian power, until the edifice itself collapsed in ruin.

To the congratulations of his friends, who entreated him to take a rest, he replied "that he had now to consider how he should begin the war against Carthage ; for up to now the Carthaginians had been making war on the Romans, but now fortune had given the Romans the opportunity of making war on the Carthaginians."

Although it must still be some time before he could convert the Roman Senate to his strategy, he set about preparing the ground. Masinissa, after the defeat at Ilipa, had come over to the Roman side, and was despatched to Africa to induce the Numidians to follow his lead. Further, Scipio sent Lælius on an embassy to sound Syphax, King of the Massæsylians, whose territory embraced most of what is to-day Algeria. Syphax, while expressing his willingness to break with Carthage, refused to ratify any treaty except with Scipio in person.

Though promised a safe conduct, the hazard of such a journey was immense. Diplomatic privileges were then in infancy, and an envoy ran risks, and not infrequently suffered a fate that was enough to chill the stoutest heart. How much greater, too, when the envoy was Rome's one victorious leader, the man whose existence was an ever-growing menace to Carthage and her allies, and who was now asked to entrust himself, far from his army, to the care of a dubious neutral. Yet this risk Scipio, calculating the risk against the prize, took, considering that the winning over of Syphax was an essential step to the further development of his policy. After making the necessary dispositions for the protection of Spain, he sailed from Cartagena with two quinqueremes. The risk, as it proved, was even greater than he calculated. Indeed, it may be that the history of the ancient world turned on a puff of wind. For he arrived off the harbour just after Hasdrubal, driven out of Spain, had cast anchor there on his way back to Carthage. Hasdrubal had with him seven triremes, and sighting the approach of what were obviously Roman ships, he hurriedly attempted to prepare his own ships and weigh anchor, in order to overpower the two quinqueremes before they could enter the neutral harbour. But a freshening breeze helped the Roman ships to enter before Hasdrubal's fleet could sail forth, and once Scipio was inside the harbour the Carthaginians did not dare to interfere.

Hasdrubal and Scipio both then sought audience of Syphax, who was much flattered by this recognition of his importance. He invited them both to be his guests, and after some demur they overcame their scruples, and supped

E

together at Syphax's table.   In such a delicate situation, Scipio's personal charm and diplomatic gifts effected a brilliant coup.   Not only Syphax but Hasdrubal succumbed to his charm, the Carthaginian openly avowing that Scipio " appeared to him more to be admired for the qualities he displayed on a personal interview with him than for his exploits in war, and that he had no doubt that Syphax and his kingdom were already at the disposal of the Romans, such was the knack that man possessed for gaining the esteem of others."   Hasdrubal was a true prophet, for Scipio sailed back with the treaty ratified.

CHAPTER VI.

THE SUBJUGATION OF SPAIN.

SCIPIO had ploughed the ground and sown the seeds for his African campaign. The time for reaping its fruits was not yet, however. He had first to complete the subjugation of Spain, and to deal out punishment to those tribes who had forsaken Rome in her hour of crisis on the Peninsula, after the death of the elder Scipios. Their heir had been too shrewd a diplomatist to show his hand earlier while the scales still hung in the balance, but now, with the Carthaginian power finally broken, it was essential for the future security of the Roman power that such treachery should not pass without retribution. The two chief offenders were Illiturgis and Castulo, cities in the neighbourhood of the battlefield of Bæcula, on the upper reaches of the Bætis (Guadalquiver). Sending a third of his forces under Marcius to deal with Castulo, he himself moved with the remainder on Illiturgis. A guilty conscience is an alert sentinel, and Scipio arrived to find that the Illiturgi had made every preparation for defence without awaiting any declaration of hostilities. He thereupon prepared to assault, dividing his army into two parts, giving command of one to Lælius, in order that they might "attack the city in two places simultaneously, thus creating an alarm in two quarters at the same time" (Livy). Here again it is interesting to note how consistently Scipio executes a convergent assault—his force divided into independently manœuvring parts to effect surprise and strain the enemy's defence, yet combining on a common objective. How strongly does his appreciation of this, the essential formula of tactics, contrast with its rarity in ancient warfare, in modern also, for how often do commanders wreck their plan either on the Scylla of a divided objective or on the Charybdis of a feint or "holding" attack to divert the enemy's attention and reserves from their main blow.

His plan made, Scipio, realising the soldiers' inherently lesser ardour against mere insurgents, strove to stimulate their determination by playing on their feelings for their betrayed comrades. He reminded them that the need for a salutary vengeance ought to make them fight more fiercely than against the Carthaginians. "For with the latter the struggle was for empire and glory almost without any exasperation, while they

had now to punish perfidy and cruelty." Such
an urge was needful, for the men of Illiturgis,
fighting with the courage of despair, with no
hope but to sell their lives as dearly as possible,
repulsed assault after assault. Indeed, because
of the circumstances that Scipio had evidently
foreseen, the previously victorious army "showed
such a want of resolution as was not very honourable to it." At this crisis, Scipio, like Napoleon
at the bridge of Lodi, did not hesitate to stake
his own life. "Considering it incumbent upon
him to exert himself in person and share the
danger, he reproved his soldiers for their cowardice, and ordered the scaling ladders to be brought
up again, threatening to mount the wall himself
since the rest hesitated." "He had now advanced near the walls with no small danger,
when a shout was raised from all sides by the
soldiers, alarmed at the danger to which their
leader was exposed, and the scaling ladders were
raised in several places at once." This fresh
impulse, coinciding with Lælius's pressure elsewhere, turned the scales, and the walls were
captured. During the resultant confusion the
citadel, too, fell to an assault on a side where
it was thought impregnable.

The treachery of Illiturgis was then avenged
in a manner so drastic as to be an object-lesson
of its requital, the inhabitants put to the sword,

and the city itself razed to the ground. Here apparently Scipio made no attempt to restrain the fury of the troops, though, as he was to show on the morrow of Zama, he could be generous beyond comparison to an open foe. In all his acts he evidently envisaged the future, and even in allowing the obliteration of Illiturgis he had a direct purpose. For the news so shook the defenders of Castulo, an obstacle made the more formidable because the garrison had been reinforced by the remains of the Carthaginian forces, that the Spanish commander, throwing over his allies, secretly capitulated. The moral purpose of the Illiturgis sack thus accomplished, Castulo escaped more lightly.

Then, sending Marcius to clear up the few remaining centres of disaffection, Scipio returned to Cartagena to pay his vows to the gods, and to give a gladiatorial show in memory of his father and uncle. This deserves passing mention, for whether due to chance or, as seems more likely, to Scipio's taste, its nature was different from the normal contest. Instead of the gladiators being slaves or captives, doomed to fight "to make a Roman holiday," they were all voluntary and unpaid, either picked representatives of tribes or soldiers anxious to show their prowess in compliment to their general or for desire of glory. Nor were they all of obscure position, but included several men of distinction, so that these games at Cartagena might be considered the birthplace of the mediæval tourney. Some, too, used it as a means to settle personal disputes, forecasting that still later development, the duel.

It was shortly after this that deserters arrived at Cartagena from Gades, offering to betray to Scipio this last stronghold of the Carthaginian power in Spain, where Mago had collected ships, fugitive troops from outlying garrisons in Spain, and auxiliaries from the African coast across the straits.   The opportunity was one not to be missed by Scipio, and he at once despatched Marcius " with the light cohorts " and Lælius " with seven triremes and one quinquereme, in order that they might act in concert by land and sea " (Livy).   Apart from the light these few words shed on Scipio's grasp of the advantage of combined land and sea operations, already made evident at Cartagena, the specific mention of " light cohorts " would seem to have a significance.   From Cartagena to Gades is a full four hundred miles.   To detach light troops, purely, for a move of this range—a landmark in military evolution—suggests Scipio's appreciation not only of the time factor, but also of the advantage of a highly mobile striking force in situations where rapidity was the coping-stone on opportunity.

The likelihood also is that he intended to follow with his legions ; but if so, this and his plans in general were upset by a severe illness, which laid him low. Exaggerated by rumour, reports that he was dead soon spread throughout the land, causing such commotion that "neither did the allies keep their allegiance nor the army their duty."

Mandonius and Andobales, dissatisfied because after the expulsion of the Carthaginians the Romans had not obligingly walked out and left them in possession, raised the standard of revolt, and began harassing the territory of the tribes faithful to the Roman alliance. As so often in history, the disappearance of the oppressor was the signal for dependencies to find the presence of their protector irksome. Mandonius and Andobales were but the forerunners of the American colonists and the modern Egyptians. There is no bond so irksome as that of gratitude.

But the menace of the situation was made more acute through the mutiny of the Roman troops themselves at Sucro, midway on the line of communication between Cartagena and Tarraco. It is a truism that line of communication troops are ever the least reliable, the most prone to discontent and disorder. Lack of employment, lack of plunder, were aggravated in this case by lack of pay, which had fallen into arrears. Be-

ginning at first with mere disregard of orders
and neglect of duty, the men soon broke out into
open mutiny, and, driving the tribunes out of
the camp, set up in command two common
soldiers, Albius and Atrius, who had been the
chief instigators of the trouble.

The mutineers had anticipated that with the
general disturbance resulting from Scipio's death,
they would be able to plunder and exact tribute
at will, while escaping notice to a large extent.
But when the rumour of Scipio's death was
refuted, the movement was, if not quenched, at
least damped down. They were in this more
subdued frame of mind when seven military
tribunes arrived, sent by Scipio. These, evidently
under instructions, took a mild line, inquiring
as to their grievances instead of upbraiding them,
and speaking to them by groups rather than
attempting to address an assembly, where the
mob spirit has full play at the expense of reason.

Polybius, and Livy clearly following him, tells
us that Scipio, experienced as he was in war but
not in dealing with sedition, felt great anxiety
and perplexity. If this be so, his course of
action does not suggest it. For a novice, or,
indeed, for a veteran commander, his handling
of the situation was a masterpiece of blended
judgment, tact, and decision. He had sent
collectors round to gather in the contributions

levied on the various cities for the army's maintenance, and took care to let it be known that this was to adjust the arrears of pay. Then he issued a proclamation that the soldiers should come to Carthage to receive their pay, in a body or in detached parties as they wished. At the same time he ordered the army at Carthage to prepare to march against Mandonius and Andobales. These chiefs, incidentally, had withdrawn within their own borders on hearing that Scipio was definitely alive. Thus the mutineers on the one hand felt themselves stripped of possible allies, and on the other, were emboldened to venture to Cartagena by the prospect of pay and, still more, of the army's departure. They took the precaution, however, to come in a body.

The seven tribunes who had inquired into their grievances were sent to meet them, with secret instructions to single out the ringleaders, and invite them to their own quarters to sup. The mutineers arrived at Cartagena at sunset, and while encouraged by the sight of the army's preparations to march, their suspicions were also lulled by their reception, being greeted as if they made a timely arrival to relieve the departing troops. These marched out, according to orders, at daybreak with their baggage, but on reaching the gate were halted and their baggage dumped. Then, promptly, guards were told off to bar all the exits from the camp, and the rest of the troops to surround the mutineers. Meanwhile the latter had been summoned to an assembly, a summons which they obeyed the more readily because they imagined that the camp, and, indeed, the general himself, were at their mercy.

Their first shock was when they saw their general vigorous and full of health, far from the sick man they had supposed, and their second followed when, after a disconcerting silence, he addressed them in a manner strangely inconsistent with the apparent insecurity of his position. Livy purports to give this speech word for word and at great length, and in his rendering it is a masterpiece of oratory and of style. Polybius's is shorter and crisper, more natural too, and is prefaced by the remark that Scipio " began to speak somewhat as follows." The lover of literature will prefer Livy's version ; but the historian, weighing the evidence of date and circumstance, will prefer to accept Polybius's version, and that as giving the general sense rather than the exact words of Scipio.

Despite these doubts, we will quote Livy for the opening phrases, because they are so telling, and because it is not unlikely that such a beginning might have been recorded with some exactitude. Saying that he was at a loss how to address them, he proceeded : " Can I call you countrymen, who have revolted from your country ?   Or soldiers, who have rejected the command and authority of your general, and violated your solemn oath ?   Can I call you enemies ? I recognise the persons, faces, and dress, and mien of fellow-countrymen ; but I perceive the actions, expressions, and intentions of enemies. For what have you wished and hoped for, but what the Illitergi and Lacetani did ? " Next he expresses wonderment as to what grievance or what expectations had led them to revolt. If it is simply a grievance over delays of pay, caused by his illness, is such action—jeopardising their country—justified, especially as they have always been paid in full since he assumed command ?   " Mercenary troops may, indeed, sometimes be pardoned for revolting against their employers, but no pardon can be extended to those who are fighting for themselves and their wives and children.   For that is just as if a man who said he had been wronged by his own father over money matters were to take up arms to kill him who was the author of his life " (Polybius).   If the cause is not merely a grievance, is it because they hoped for more profit and plunder by taking service with the enemy ?   If so, who would be their possible allies ?   Men like Andobales and Mandonius ; a fine thing to put their trust in such repeated turncoats !

Then he turns his scorn on the leaders they have chosen, ignorant and baseborn, parodying their names, Atrius and Albius—" Blackie " and " Whitie,"—and so appealing to their sense of the ridiculous and their superstition.   He throws in a grim reminder of the legion which revolted at Rhegium, and for it suffered beheading to the last man.   But even these put themselves under command of a military tribune.   What hope of successful revolt could they have entertained ? Even had the rumour of his death been correct, did they imagine that such tried leaders as Silanus, Lælius, or Scipio's brother could have failed to avenge the insult to Rome ?

When he has shattered their confidence and stimulated their fears by such telling arguments, the way is paved for him to detach them from the instigators of the revolt and to win back their loyalty.   Changing his tone from harshness to gentleness, he continues : " I will plead for you to Rome and to myself, using a plea universally acknowledged among men—that all multitudes are easily misled and easily impelled to excesses, so that a multitude is ever liable to the same changes as the sea.   For as the sea is by its own nature harmless to voyagers and quiet, yet when agitated by winds it appears of the same turbulent character as the winds, so a multitude ever appears to be and actually is of the same character as the leaders and counsellors it happens to have." In Livy's version he makes also a deftly sympathetic comparison, well calculated to touch their hearts, between his own recent sickness of body and their sickness of mind. " Therefore I, too, on the present occasion . . . consent to be reconciled to you, and grant you an amnesty. But with the guilty instigators of revolt we refuse to be reconciled, and have decided to punish for their offences. . . ." As he finished speaking, the loyal troops, who had encircled the assembly, clashed their swords on their shields to strike terror into the mutineers ; the herald's voice was heard citing by name the condemned agitators ; and these offenders were brought bound and naked into the midst of the assembly, and then executed in the sight of all. It was a perfectly timed and concerted plan, and the mutineers were too cowed to raise a hand or utter a protest. The punishment carried out, the mass received assurance of forgiveness, and took a fresh oath of loyalty to the tribunes. By a characteristic touch of Scipio's, each man received his full demand of pay as he answered his name.

This masterly handling of a gravely menacing situation has more than a reminder of Pétain's methods in quelling the mutinies of 1917—had the great Frenchman perchance studied the

mutiny of Sucro ?—not only in its blend of
severity to ringleaders with the just rectification
of grievances, but in the way the moral health
of the body military was restored with the least
possible use of the knife. This was true economy
of force, for it meant that the eight thousand
became not merely unwilling reinforcements,
cowed into acquiescence with orders, but loyal
supporters.

But the suppression of this mutiny was only
one step towards restoring the situation caused
by Scipio's illness. The expedition against
Gades had been abortive, primarily because the
plot had been discovered by the Carthaginian
commander, and the conspirators arrested.
Though they won local successes, Lælius and
Marcius found Gades prepared, and so, forced
to abandon their project, returned to Cartagena.

There Scipio was about to march against the
Spanish rebels. In ten days he reached the
Ebro, a full three hundred miles, and four days
later pitched his camp within sight of the enemy.
A circular valley lay between the two camps,
and into this he drove some cattle protected only
by light troops, to " excite the rapacity of the
barbarians." At the same time he placed Lælius
with the cavalry in concealment behind a spur.
The bait succeeded, and while the rival skirmishers
were merrily engaged, Lælius emerged from cover,

part of his cavalry charging the Spanish in front, and the other part riding round the foot of the hill to cut them off from their camp. The consequent reverse so irritated the Spanish that next morning at daybreak their army marched out to offer battle.

This suited Scipio excellently, for the valley was so confined that the Spanish by this act committed themselves to a cramped close quarter combat on the level, where the peculiar aptitude of the Romans in hand-to-hand fighting gave them an initial advantage over troops more adapted to hill fighting at longer ranges. And, furthermore, in order to find room for their horse they were forced to leave one-third of their foot out of the battle, stationed on the slope behind.

The conditions suggested a fresh expedient to Scipio. The valley was so narrow that the Spanish could not post their cavalry on the flanks of the infantry line, which took up the whole space. Seeing this, Scipio realised that his own infantry flanks were automatically secured, and accordingly sent Lælius with the cavalry round by the hills in a wide turning movement. Then, ever alive to the vital importance of securing his intended manœuvre by a vigorous fixing attack, he himself advanced into the valley with his infantry, with four cohorts in front, this being the most he could effectively deploy on the narrow front. This thrust, as he intended, occupied the attention of the Spanish, and prevented them from observing the cavalry manœuvre until the blow fell, and they heard the noise of the cavalry engagement in their rear. Thus the Spanish were forced to fight two separate battles, their cavalry neither able to aid their infantry, nor the infantry their cavalry, and each doomed to the demoralising sound of conflict in their rear, so that each action had a moral reaction on the other.

Cramped and assailed by skilled close-quarter fighters, whose formation gave them the advantage of depth for successive blows, the Spanish infantry were cut to pieces. Then the Spanish cavalry, surrounded, suffering the pressure of the fugitives, the direct attack of the Roman infantry, and the rear attack of the Roman cavalry, could not use their mobility, and, forced to a standing fight, were slain to the last man after a gallant but hopeless resistance. It is a testimony to the fierceness of the fight and to the quality of the Spanish resistance, when hope had gone, that the Roman losses were twelve hundred killed and over three thousand wounded. Of the Spanish the only survivors were the light-armed third of their force who had remained on the hill, idle spectators of the tragedy in the

F

valley.   These, along with their chiefs, fled in time.

This decisive triumph was a fitting conclusion to Scipio's Spanish campaigns—campaigns which for all their long neglect by military students reveal a profound grasp of strategy—at a time when strategy had hardly been born,—and of its intimate relation to policy.   But, above all, they deserve to be immortalised for their richness of tactical achievement.   Military history hardly contains such another series of ingenious and inspired battle manœuvres, surpassing on balance even those of Hannibal in Italy.   If Scipio profited by Hannibal's unintended course of instruction on the battlefields of Italy, the pupil surpassed even the master.   Nor does such a probability diminish Scipio's credit, for the highest part of the art of war is inborn, not acquired, or why did not later captains, ancient and modern, profit more by Scipio's demonstrations.   Wonderful as was Hannibal's fertility of plan, there appears in Scipio's record a still richer variety, a still more complete calculation, and in three directions a definite superiority. The attack on a fortified place was admittedly in Hannibal a weakness ; in Scipio the reverse, for Cartagena is a landmark in history.   The pursuit after Ilipa marks a new advance in warfare, as also the wide concealed turning movement in this last battle against Andobales, a development clearly beyond the narrow outflanking manœuvres which had hitherto been the high-water mark of tactical skill.

Scipio's military motto would seem to have been " every time a new stratagem." Has ever a general been so fertile an artist of war ? Beside him most of the celebrated captains of history appear mere dabblers in the art, showing in their whole career but one or two variations of orthodox practice. And be it remembered that with one exception Scipio's triumphs were won over first-class opponents ; not, like Alexander, over Asiatic mobs; like Cæsar, over tribal hordes; or like Frederick and Napoleon, over the courtier-generals and senile pedants of an atrophied military system.

This victory over Andobales and Mandonius proved to be the coping-stone not only on his military career in Spain, but on the political conquest of the country. So decisive had it been that Andobales realised the futility of further resistance, and sent his brother Mandonius to sue for peace unconditionally. One imagines that Mandonius must have felt some pessimism as to his reception and as to his tenure of life. It would have been natural to have dealt out to these twice-repeated rebels a dire vengeance. But Scipio knew human nature, including Spanish nature. No vengeance could improve his military or political position, now unchallenged, whereas, on the other hand, it would merely sow the seeds of future trouble, convert the survivors into embittered foes, biding their time for a fresh outbreak. Little as he counted on their fidelity, generosity was the one course which might secure it. Therefore, after upbraiding Mandonius, and through him, Andobales, driving home the helplessness of their position and the rightful forfeiture of their lives, he made a peace as generous as it was diplomatically foresighted. To show how little he feared them, he did not demand the surrender of their arms and all their possessions, as was the custom, nor even the required hostages, saying that " should they revolt, he would not take vengeance on their unoffending hostages, but upon themselves, inflicting punishment not upon defenceless but on armed enemies " (Livy). The wisdom of this policy found its justification in the fact that from this juncture Spain disappears from the history of the Punic War, whether as a base of recruitment and supply for the Carthaginian armies or as a distraction from Scipio's concentration on his new objective —Carthage itself. True, revolts broke out at intervals, the first avowedly from the contempt

GALLIA

CANTABRI

PYRENÆI MONTES

ILERGETES

BARCINO

TARRACO

IBERUS FL.

IBERUS FL.

IBERUS FL.

CELTIBERI

SAGUNTUM

SUCRO

CARPETANI

VETTONES

TAGUS FL.

LUSITANI

ANAS FL.

CASTULONENSIS
SALTUS
CASTULO
BAECULA
ILITURGIS
BAETIS FL.
ILIPA

BAETICA

CARTHAGO
NOVA

CALPE M.
(HERCULIS COLUMNA)

BAETIS FL.

GADES

OCEANUS

ATLANTICUS

MARE   INTERNUM

MINOR

BALEARES INS.

MAJOR

PITYUSÆ I.

SPAIN
(AT TIME OF 2ND PUNIC WAR)

BRITISH MILES
0   25   50   75   100

felt by the Spanish for the generals who succeeded Scipio, and recurred for centuries. But
they were isolated and spasmodic outbursts, and
limited to the hill tribes, in whose blood fighting
was a malarial fever.

Scipio's mission in Spain was accomplished.
Only Gades held out as the last fragment of the
Carthaginian power, and this, being then an
island fortress, was impregnable save through
possible betrayal by its defenders. By some
historians Mago's escape from Gades is made
an imputation on Scipio's generalship, yet from
a comparison of the authorities it would seem
probable that Mago left there, under orders from
Carthage, while Scipio was occupied with the
far more pressing menace of the mutiny and
Andobales's revolt. Mago, too, was not such a
redoubtable personality that his departure, with
a handful of troops, for other fields was in itself
a menace to the general situation, even if it
could have been prevented, which militarily was
impossible. Actually, on his voyage from Gades,
he attempted a surprise assault on Cartagena in
the absence of Scipio, and was so easily repulsed
and so strongly counter-attacked, that the ships
cut their anchors in order to avoid being boarded,
leaving many of the defeated soldiers to drown
or be slain. Forced to return to Gades to recruit

afresh, he was refused entry to the city by the inhabitants, who shortly surrendered to the Romans, and had to retrace his course to the island of Pityusa (modern Iviça), the western-most of the Balearic Isles, which was inhabited by Carthaginians. After receiving recruits and supplies, he attempted a landing on Majorca, but was repulsed by the natives, famous as slingers, and had to choose the less advantageous site of Minorca as his winter quarters, there hauling his ships on shore.

With regard to the chronology of this last phase, in Livy's account the suppression of Andobales's rebellion is followed by the story of a meeting between Scipio and Masinissa, and then by the details of Mago's departure from Gades, from which it would appear that this happened while Scipio was still in Spain. But for accuracy of historical sequence Livy is a less reliable guide than Polybius, and the latter's narrative definitely states that directly after the subjugation of Andobales Scipio returned to Tarraco, and then, "anxious not to arrive in Rome too late for the consular elections," sailed for Rome, after handing over the army to Silanus and Marcius, and arranging for the administration of the province.

The meeting with Masinissa, whenever it occurred, is worth notice, for here the seeds of Scipio's generous treatment of Masinissa's nephew years before bore fruit in the exchange of pledges of an alliance, which was to be one of Scipio's master-tools in undermining the Carthaginian power at its base in Africa.

CHAPTER VII.

THE TRUE OBJECTIVE.

ON arrival at Rome Scipio obtained an audience
of the Senate outside the city, at the temple of
Bellona, and there gave them a formal report
of his campaigns. " On account of these services
he rather tried his prospect of a triumph than
pressed it pertinaciously," for the honour had
never been given except to those whose services
were rendered when holders of a magistracy.
His tact was wise, for the astonishing success of
youth had already inspired envy among his
seniors. The Senate did not break with prece-
dent, and at the close of the audience he entered
the city in the ordinary way. His reward, however, came without delay. At the assembly for
the election of the two consuls for the coming
year he was named by all the centuries. The
popularity of his election was shown not only
by the enthusiasm which greeted it, but by the
gathering of a larger number of voters than at
any time during the Punic War, crowds swarm-

ing to his house and to the Capitol full of curiosity to see the victor of the Spanish wars.

But on the morrow of this personal triumph, compensation for the formal " triumph " denied him by a hidebound Senate, the first shoots appeared of that undergrowth of narrow-minded conservatism, reinforced by envy, which was to choke the personal fruits of his work, though happily not before he had garnered for Rome the first-fruits—Hannibal's overthrow.

Hitherto in Spain he had enjoyed a free hand unfettered by jealous politicians or the compromising counsels of government by committee. If he had to rely on his own local resources, he was at least too far distant for his essential freedom of action to be controlled by any many-headed guardian of national policy. But from now on he was to suffer, like Marlborough and Wellington some two thousand years later, the curb of political faction and jealousy, and finally, like Marlborough, end his days in embittered retirement. The report got about that he was saying that he had been declared consul not merely to prosecute, but to finish the war ; that for this object it was essential for him to move with his army into Africa ; and that if the Senate opposed this plan he would carry it through with the people's backing, overriding the Senate. Perhaps his friends were indiscreet; perhaps Scipio himself, so old beyond his years in other ways, allowed youthful confidence to outride his discretion; perhaps, most probable of all, he knew the Senate's innate narrowness of vision and had been sounding the people's opinion.

The upshot was, that when the question was raised in the Senate, Fabius Cunctator voiced the conservative view. The man who had worthily won his name by inaction, his natural caution reinforced by an old man's jealousy, cleverly if spitefully criticises the plan of a young man whose action threatens to eclipse his fame. First, he points out that neither had the Senate voted nor the people ordered that Africa should be constituted a consul's province this year, insinuating that if the consul came before them with his mind already made up, such conduct is an insult to them. Next, Fabius seeks to parry any imputation of jealousy by dwelling on his own past achievements as if they were too exalted for any possible feats of Scipio to threaten comparison. How characteristic, too, of age the remark, "What rivalry can there exist between myself and a man who is not equal in years even to my son?" He urges that Scipio's duty is to attack Hannibal in Italy. "Why do you not apply yourself to this, and carry the war in a straightforward manner to the place where Han-

nibal is, rather than pursue that roundabout
course, according to which you expect that when
you have crossed into Africa Hannibal will follow
you thither." How vivid is the reminder here
of Eastern *v.* Western controversy in the war of
1914-1918. " What if Hannibal should advance
against Rome ? " How familiar to modern ears
is this argument employed against any military
heretic who questions the doctrine of Clausewitz
that the enemy's main army is the primary
military objective.

Fabius then insinuates that Scipio's head has
been turned by his successes in Spain. These
Fabius damns with faint praise and covert sneers
—sneers which Mommsen and other modern
historians seem to have accepted as literal truth,
forgetting how decisively all Fabius's arguments
were refuted by Scipio's actions. How different,
Fabius contends, is the problem Scipio will have
to face if he ventures to Africa. Not a harbour
open, not even a foothold already secured, not
an ally. Does Scipio trust his hold over Masinissa when he could not trust even his own
soldiers ?—a jibe at the Sucro mutiny. Land in
Africa, and he will rally the whole land against
him, all internal disputes forgotten in face of
the foreign foe. Even in the unlikely event of
forcing Hannibal's return, how much worse will
it be to face him near Carthage, supported by all

Africa, instead of with a remnant in Southern Italy ? "What sort of policy is that of yours, to prefer fighting where your own forces will be diminished by one-half, and the enemy's greatly augmented ? "

Fabius finishes with a scathing comparison of Scipio with his father, who, setting out for Spain, returned to Italy to meet Hannibal, "while you are going to leave Italy when Hannibal is there, not because you consider such a course beneficial to the State, but because you think it will redound to your honour and glory . . . the armies were enlisted for the protection of the city and of Italy, and not for the consuls, like kings, to carry into whatever part of the world they please from motives of vanity."

This speech makes a strong impression on the Senators, "especially those advanced in years," and when Scipio rises to reply the majority are clearly against him.   His opening is an apt counter-thrust : " Even Quintus Fabius himself has observed . . . that in the opinion he gave a feeling of jealousy might be suspected.   And though I dare not myself charge so great a man with harbouring that feeling, yet, whether it is owing to a defect in his phrasing, or to the fact, that suspicion has certainly not been removed. For he has so magnified his own honours and the fame of his exploits, to do away with the imputation of envy, that it would appear I am in danger of being rivalled by every obscure person, but not by himself, because he enjoys an eminence above everybody else. . . ." "He has represented himself as an old man, and as one who has gone through every gradation of honour, and me as below the age even of his son, as if he supposed that the desire of glory did not exceed the span of life, and as if its chief part had no respect to memory and future ages." Then, with gentle sarcasm Scipio refers to Fabius's expressed solicitude for his safety, and not only for the army and the State, should he cross over to Africa. Whence has this concern so suddenly sprung ? When his father and uncle were slain, when Spain lay beneath the heel of four victorious Carthaginian armies, when no one except himself would offer themselves for such a forlorn venture, "why was it that no one at that time made any mention of my age, of the strength of the enemy, of the difficulties, of the recent fate of my father and uncle ? " "Are there now larger armies in Africa, more and better generals, than were then in Spain ? Was my age then more mature for conducting a war than now . . .? " "After having routed four Carthaginian armies . . . after having regained possession of the whole of Spain, so that no trace of war remains, it is an easy matter to

make light of my services ; just as easy as it
would be, should I return from Africa, to make
light of those very conditions which are now
magnified for the purpose of detaining me here."
Then, after demolishing the historical examples
which Fabius had quoted as warnings, Scipio
makes this appeal to history recoil against Fabius
by adducing Hannibal's example in support of
his plan. " He who brings danger upon another
has more spirit than he who repels it. Add to
this, that the terror excited by the unexpected
is increased thereby. When you have entered
the territory of an enemy you obtain a near
view of his strong and weak points." After
pointing out the moral " soft spots " in Africa,
Scipio continues : " Provided no impediment is
caused here, you will hear at once that I have
landed, and that Africa is blazing with war ;
that Hannibal is preparing to depart from this
country." " . . . Many things which are not
now apparent at this distance will develop ; and
it is the part of a general not to be wanting
when opportunity arises, and to bend its events
to his designs. I shall, Quintus Fabius, have
the opponent you assign me, Hannibal, but
I shall rather draw him after me than be kept
here by him." As for the danger of a move
by Hannibal on Rome, it is a poor compliment
to Crassus, the other consul, to suppose that

he will not be able to keep Hannibal's reduced
and shaken forces in check, when Fabius did so
with Hannibal at the height of his power and
success—an unanswerable master-thrust this !

After emphasising that now is the time and
the opportunity to turn the tables on Carthage,
to do to Africa what Hannibal did to Italy,
Scipio ends on a characteristic note of restraint
and exaltation combined : " Though Fabius has
depreciated my services in Spain, I will not
attempt to turn his glory into ridicule and
magnify my own. If in nothing else, though
a young man, I will show my superiority over
this old man in modesty and in the government
of my tongue. Such has been my life, and such
the services I have performed, that I can rest
content in silence with that opinion which you
have spontaneously formed of me."

The Senate, however, were more concerned
with the preservation of their own privileges
than with the military arguments, and demanded
to know if Scipio would leave the decision with
them, or, if they refused, appeal, over their
heads, to the people's verdict. They refused to
give a decision until they had an assurance that
he would abide by it. After a consultation with
his colleague, Scipio gave way to this demand.
Thereupon the Senate, a typical committee,
effected a compromise by which the consul to

whose lot Sicily fell might have permission to cross into Africa if he judged it to be for the advantage of the State. Curiously, Sicily fell to Scipio !

He took with him thirty warships, which by great energy he had built and launched within forty-five days of the timber being taken from the woods ; of these twenty were quinqueremes and ten quadriremes. On board he embarked seven thousand volunteers, as the Senate, afraid to block him but keen to obstruct him, had refused him leave to levy troops.

The story of how, beset with difficulties and hampered by those he was aiming to save, he took this unorganised band of volunteers and trained it to be the nucleus of an effective expeditionary force finds a notable parallel in our own history. Sicily was to be Scipio's Shorncliffe Camp, the place where he forged the weapon that was to be thrust at the heart of Carthage. But Scipio, unlike Sir John Moore in the Napoleonic War, was himself to handle the weapon his genius had created, and with it to strike the death-blow at Hannibal's power. His vision penetrating the distant future, a quality in which he perhaps surpasses all other great commanders, enabled him to realise that the tactical key to victory lay in the possession of a superior mobile arm of decision—cavalry. It is not the least

tribute to his genius that to appreciate this he
had to break loose from the fetters of a great
tradition, for Rome's military greatness was
essentially built on the power of her legionary
infantry. The long and splendid annals of
Roman history are the testimony to its effective-
ness, and only in Scipio's brief passage across the
stage do we find a real break with this tradition,
a balance between the two arms by which the
power of the one for fixing and of the other for
decisive manœuvre are proportioned and combined. It is an object-lesson to modern general
staffs, shivering on the brink of mechanicalisa-
tion, fearful of the plunge despite the proved
ineffectiveness of the older arms in their present
form, for no military tradition has been a tithe
so enduring and so resplendent as that of
the legion. From his arrival in Sicily onwards
Scipio bent his energies to developing a superior
cavalry, and Zama, where Hannibal's decisive
weapon was turned against himself, is Scipio's
justification.

How unattainable must this goal have seemed
when he landed in Sicily with a mere seven thousand heterogeneous volunteers. Yet within a
few days the first progress was recorded. At
once organising his volunteers into cohorts and
centuries, Scipio kept aside three hundred of
the pick. One can imagine their perplexed

G

wonder at being left without arms and not told off to centuries like their comrades.

Next he nominated three hundred of the noblest born Sicilian youths to accompany him to Africa, and appointed a day on which they were to present themselves equipped with horses and arms. The honour of nomination for such a hazardous venture affrighted both them and their parents, and they paraded most reluctantly. Addressing them, Scipio remarked that he had heard rumours of their aversion to this arduous service, and rather than take unwilling comrades he would prefer that they would openly avow their feelings. One of them immediately seized this loophole of escape, and Scipio thereupon released him from service and promised to provide a substitute on condition that he handed over his horse and arms and trained his substitute in their handling. The Sicilian joyfully accepted, and the rest, seeing that the general did not take his action amiss, promptly followed his example. By this means Scipio obtained a nucleus of picked Roman cavalry " at no expense to the State."

His next measures show not only how his every step tended towards his ultimate object, but also how alive he was to the importance of foresight in securing his future action. He sent Lælius on an advance reconnoitring expedition to Africa, and in order not to impair the resources he was building up repaired his old ships for this expedition, hauling his new ones upon shore for the winter at Panormus, as they had been hastily and inevitably built of unseasoned timber. Further, after distributing his army through the towns, he ordered the Sicilian States to furnish corn for the troops, saving up the corn which he had brought with him from Italy—economy of force even in the details of supply. Scipio knew that strategy depends on supply, that without security of food the most dazzling manœuvres may come to nought.

Furthermore, an offensive, whether strategical or tactical, must operate from a secure base—this is one of the cardinal axioms of war. " Basis " would perhaps be a better term, for " base " is apt to be construed too narrowly, whereas truly it comprises security to the geographical base, both internal and external, as well as security of supply and of movement. Napoleon in 1814, the Germans in 1918, both suffered the dislocation of their offensive action through the insecurity of their base internally. It is thus interesting to note how Scipio sought among his preparatory measures to ensure this security. He found Sicily, and especially Syracuse, suffering from internal discontent and disorder which had arisen out of the war. The property of the

Syracusans had been seized after the famous siege by covetous Romans and Italians, and despite the decrees of the Senate for its restitution, had never been handed back. Scipio took an early opportunity of going to Syracuse, and " deeming it of the first importance to maintain trust in Rome's plighted word," restored their property to the citizens, by proclamation and even by direct action against those who still clung fast to the plundered property. This act of justice had a wide effect throughout Sicily, and not only ensured the tranquillity of his base but won the active support of the Sicilians in furnishing his forces for the expedition.

Meanwhile Lælius had landed at Hippo Regius (modern Bona), about 150 miles distant from Carthage. According to Livy the news threw Carthage into a panic, the citizens believing that Scipio himself had landed with his army, and anticipating an immediate march on Carthage. To ward this off seemed hopeless, as their own people were untrained for war, their mercenary troops of doubtful loyalty, and among the African chiefs Syphax was alienated from them since his conference with Scipio, and Masinissa a declared enemy. The panic did not abate until news came that the invader was Lælius, not Scipio, and that his forces were only strong enough for a raid. Livy further tells us that the Carthaginians took advantage of the respite to send embassies to Syphax and others of the African chiefs for the purpose of strengthening their alliance, and envoys were also sent to Hannibal and Mago to urge them to keep Scipio at home by playing on the fears of the Romans. Mago had, earlier, landed at Genoa, but was too weak to act effectively, and to encourage him to move towards Rome and join Hannibal, the Carthaginian Senate sent him seven thousand troops and also money to hire auxiliaries.

If these facts be true, they would on the surface suggest that Scipio lost an opportunity and was unwise to put the Carthaginians on their guard by this raid of Lælius's, and this impression is strengthened by the words ascribed to Masinissa. For Livy says that Masinissa came, with a small body of horse, to meet Lælius, and complained that "Scipio had not acted with promptness, in that he had not already passed his army over into Africa, while the Carthaginians were in consternation, and while Syphax was entangled in wars with neighbouring States, and in doubt as to the side he should take ; that if Syphax was allowed time to settle his own affairs, he would not keep faith with the Romans." Masinissa then begged that Lælius would urge Scipio not to delay, promising that he, though driven from his kingdom, would join Scipio with a force of horse and foot.

When, however, we appreciate the situation from a military angle it appears in a different light. Lælius landed at the port which was nearest to Numidia, and which was not only 150 miles distant from Carthage, but with a wide belt of hill country intervening. When Scipio himself landed it was at a spot only some twenty-five .miles distant. Hence Lælius's expedition can have been in no sense a reconnaissance against Carthage, and the clear deduction is that it was a reconnaissance to discover the state and feeling of the African States where Scipio hoped to find allies, and in particular to get in touch with Masinissa. As we have shown, Scipio had realised that a superiority in the cavalry arm was the key to victory over the Carthaginians, and he looked to the Numidian chief for his main source. His appreciation of the latter's brilliant cavalry leadership on the battlefields of Spain had inspired him to win Masinissa over. Thus the inherent probability is that Lælius's mission was primarily to discover if the Numidian would actually hold to his new alliance when Roman troops landed on African soil, and if so, what were the resources he could contribute. If the Carthaginians were really panic-stricken at a raid so distant, the fact but

helped to confirm Scipio's view of the moral
advantage to be gained from a thrust at Carthage.
As for the warning thus given, the danger of
putting the Carthaginians on their guard, this
had already been given by Scipio's speeches in
the Senate and his preparations. Where consent
for his expedition had to be wrung from a reluc-
tant Senate, where the forces and resources for
it had to be raised without State help, strategic
surprise was out of the question from the outset.
Here were exemplified the chronic drawbacks of
a constitutional system of government for conducting war. It is one of Scipio's supreme merits
that he obtained completely decisive results,
though lacking the tremendous asset of political
control. He, the servant of a republic, is the
one exception to the rule that throughout the
history of war the most successful of the great
captains have been despots or autocrats. Count-
less historians have lavished sympathy on Hannibal for the handicap he suffered through lack
of support from home, and laid all his set-backs
at the door of the Carthaginian Senate. None
seem to have stressed Scipio's similar handicap.
Yet to Rome there was none of the physical
difficulty in sending reinforcements that Carthage
could plead as an excuse. In this lack of support—nay worse, the active opposition—from the
Roman Senate lies unquestionably the reason

of Scipio's delay of a year in Sicily to prepare
for the expedition. He had to find unaided his
own resources in Sicily and Africa. How ground-
less as well as irrational was Masinissa's complaint, if he made it, is shown by the fact that
when, in 204 B.C., Scipio landed in Africa, the
" landless prince," to quote Mommsen, " brought
in the first instance nothing beyond his personal
ability to the aid of the Romans." Few generals
have been so bold as Scipio when boldness was
the right policy, but he was too imbued with
the principle of security to strike before he had
armed himself and tempered his weapon by
training. The wonder is not at Scipio's delay
of a year, but that he moved so soon, and with
a force that in numbers if not in training was
still so puny for the scope of his task. But this
seeming audacity was made secure by his strategy
after the landing, and Zama was its justification.
It is an ironical comment on the value of their
judgments that the same historians who criticise
Scipio for his tardiness in 205 B.C., tax him with
rashness for the smallness of the force with
which he sailed in 204 B.C. ! One of these, Dodge,
when dealing with the first year, remarks that
" Scipio does not seem to have been very expedi-
tious about the business. In this he resembled
M'Clellan, as well as in his popularity." Later,

dealing with Scipio's embarkation, Dodge says: " Some generals would have declared these means insufficient ; but Scipio possessed an abundance of self-confidence which supplemented material strength in all but severe tests." Such criticism is a boomerang recoiling on the critic.

CHAPTER VIII.

A POLITICAL HITCH.

THE interval between the return of Lælius and
the embarkation for Africa is occupied, apart
from material preparation, by two episodes of
significance. The first is Scipio's apparent "side-
show" at Locri; the second, the political im-
broglio which for a time threatened his ruin and
that of his plans. Both deserve study for the
light they shed on his character as a commander
and a man.

Locri lay on the underpart of the toe of Italy
(near modern Gerace), and was in Hannibal's
possession. After his brother Hasdrubal's defeat
at the Metaurus, Hannibal had fallen back on
Bruttium, the southernmost province of Italy,
and here he held at bay the consular armies,
who dared not advance to seek out the scarred
but indomitable lion in his mountain fastnesses.

Some Locrians who had gone outside the walls
were captured by a Roman raiding party, and
taken to Rhegium—the port adjacent to Sicily,—

where they were recognised by the pro-Roman Locrian nobles, who had found sanctuary there when their town fell into Carthaginian hands. Certain of the prisoners, who were skilled artisans and had been in the employment and trust of the Carthaginians, suggested that, if ransomed, they would be willing to betray the citadel at Locri. The nobles, eager to regain their town, at once ransomed the artisans, and after concerting a plan and signals, sent them back to Locri. Then, going to Scipio at Syracuse, they told him of the scheme. He saw the opportunity, and despatched on the venture a detachment of three thousand men under two military tribunes. Exchanging signals with the conspirators inside, ladders were let down about midnight, and the attackers swarmed up the walls. Surprise magnified their strength, and the Carthaginians in confusion fled from the citadel to a second citadel on the farther side of the town. For several days encounters occurred between the two parties without decisive result. Alive to the danger to his garrison, and to the threatened loss of an important point, Hannibal moved to the rescue, sending a messenger ahead with orders to the garrison to make a sortie at daybreak as a cloak to what he hoped would be his surprise assault. He had not, however, brought scaling ladders with him, and so was forced to postpone his attack a day while he was preparing these and other materials for storming the walls.

Scipio, who was at Messana, received word of Hannibal's move, and planned a counter-surprise. Leaving his brother in command at Messana, he embarked a force, and, setting sail on the next tide, arrived in the harbour of Locri shortly before nightfall. The troops were hidden in the town during the night, a concealment made possible by the townspeople favouring, though not openly taking, the side of the Romans. Next morning Hannibal launched his assault in conjunction with the sortie from the Carthaginians' citadel. As the scaling ladders were being brought forward, Scipio sallied out from one of the town gates and attacked the Carthaginians in flank and rear. The shock of the surprise dislocated and disorganised the Carthaginians, and, his plan upset, Hannibal fell back on his own camp. Realising that the Romans, because of their grip on the town, were masters of the situation, he withdrew during the night, sending word to his garrison in the citadel to make their way out as best they could and rejoin him.

For Scipio this " side-show " was a very real asset. Apart from the personal prestige he gained from his success in this first encounter with the dreaded Hannibal, scoring a trick even off the

master of ruses, he had helped the Roman
campaign in Italy by curtailing Hannibal's remaining foothold in that country—and without
any diminution of his own force. But, beyond
these personal and indirect gains, his success
had an important bearing on his own future
plan of operations. For he had " blooded " his
troops against Hannibal, and by this successful
enterprise given them a moral tonic, which would
be of immense value in the crucial days to come.
It is unfortunate that for this episode, as for
Lælius's reconnaissance in Africa, we have no
Polybius to reveal to us the motives and calculations which inspired Scipio's moves. The
loss of Polybius's books on this period must be
replaced by deduction from the facts, and from
the knowledge already gained of Scipio's mind.
To those who have followed his constant and far-
sighted exploitation of the moral element during
his Spanish campaigns, there can be little doubt
that he seized on the Locri expedition as a heaven-
sent chance not only to test and sharpen his
weapon for the day of trial, but to dispel in his
troops the impression of Hannibalic invincibility.

The second episode arose out of the subsequent
administration of recaptured Locri. When Scipio
had sent the original force to seize the town,
he had instructed Quintus Pleminius, the pro-
prætor at Rhegium, to assist the tribunes, and

when the place was captured Pleminius, by
virtue of his seniority, assumed the command
until Scipio arrived. After the repulse of Hannibal's relieving force, Scipio returned to Sicily,
and Pleminius was naturally left in chief command of the town and its defence, though the
detachment from Sicily remained under the
direct command of the tribunes.

How Pleminius abused his trust is one of the
most sordid pages in Roman history. The
wretched inhabitants suffered worse from his
tyranny and lust than ever they had from the
Carthaginians—an ill-requital of their aid to
the Romans in regaining the town. The example
of their leader infected the troops, and their
greed for loot not only harassed the townspeople
but inevitably led to disorder among themselves.
It would seem that the tribunes strove to check
this growing license, and to uphold the true
standards of military discipline. One of Pleminius's men, running away with a silver cup that
he had stolen from a house and pursued by its
owners, met the tribunes in his flight. They
stopped him and had the cup taken away, whereat
his comrades showered abuse on the tribunes,
and the disturbance soon ended in a free fight
between the soldiers of the tribunes and those of
Pleminius. The latter were worsted and invoked
the aid of their commander, inciting him by

tales of the reproaches cast upon his behaviour and control. Pleminius thereupon ordered the tribunes to be brought before him, stripped, and beaten. During the short delay while the rods were being brought and themselves stripped, the tribunes called upon their men for aid. The latter, hastily gathering from all quarters, were so inflamed at the sight that, breaking loose from the habits of discipline, they vented their rage on Pleminius. Cutting him off from his party, they mutilated his nose and ears, and left him almost lifeless.

When word of the disturbance reached Scipio, he sailed immediately for Locri and held a court of inquiry. Of the evidence and of the reasons for his judgment we know nothing. All that is handed down is the fact that he acquitted Pleminius, restored him to command, and pronouncing the tribunes guilty, ordered them to be thrown into chains and sent back to Rome for the Senate to deal with. He then returned to Sicily.

The verdict appears somewhat astonishing, the one serious blemish, in fact, on Scipio's judgment. The motives which inspired it are difficult to surmise. Perhaps it was partly pity for the mutilated Pleminius, combined with anger that his own men should have shown such gross insubordination and committed such an atrocity.

It is a natural instinct with the best type of commander to be more severe on the misconduct of his own direct subordinates than on those who are only attached to him, and in case of dispute between the two such a man may err because of his very scrupulousness to hold the balance fairly, and to avoid partiality towards his own. It was said of one of the finest British commanders in the war of 1914-18 that if he had a personal dislike or distrust of a subordinate he invariably gave the latter more rope than the others, knowing that if his distrust was justified the man would assuredly use this rope to hang himself. Similar may have been the motives underlying Scipio's outwardly inexplicable verdict. In criticising it the historian must consider not only the gaps in our knowledge of the case, but view the incident in the general light of all Scipio's recorded acts as a commander. The whole weight of evidence, as we have seen, goes to show that two qualities which especially distinguished Scipio were the acuteness of his understanding of men, and his humanity to the conquered. Trust in a Pleminius or condonation of brutality were the last things to be expected of him, and so, lacking evidence as to the facts on which his decision was based, it would be rash to pass adverse judgment on his action.

We need to remember also that Locri was in

Italy, and therefore outside his province, and a close attention to its administration could only be at the expense of his primary object—preparation for the expedition to Africa.

The importance of the Locri incident is not as a light on Scipio's character, but as a political rock on which his military plans nearly foundered. How this came about can be briefly told. After Scipio's departure, Pleminius, who thought that the injury he had sustained had been treated too lightly by Scipio, disobeyed the latter's instructions. He had the tribunes dragged before him and tortured to death, refusing even to allow their mangled bodies to be buried. His injuries still rankling, he then sought to avenge himself by multiplying the burdens put on the Locrians. In despair, they sent a deputation to the Roman Senate. Their envoys arrived soon after the consular elections, which had marked the end of Scipio's term of office, though he was continued in command of the troops in Sicily. Their tale of misery raised a storm of popular indignation at Rome, and Scipio's senatorial opponents were not slow to divert this on to the head of the man nominally responsible. It is no surprise to find that Fabius initiated this by asking if they had carried their complaints to Scipio. The envoys replied, according to Livy, that " deputies were sent to him, but he

H

was occupied with the preparations for the war, and had either already crossed over into Africa, or was on the point of doing so." They added that his previous decision between Pleminius and the tribunes had given them the impression that the former was in favour with Scipio.

Fabius had got the answer he wanted, and after the envoys had withdrawn, hastened to condemn Scipio unheard, declaring "that he was born for the corruption of military discipline. In Spain he almost lost more men in consequence of the mutiny than in the war. That, after the manner of foreigners and kings, he indulged the licentiousness of the soldiers, and then punished them with cruelty." This envenomed speech Fabius followed up with "a resolution equally harsh." It was "that Pleminius should be conveyed to Rome in chains, and in chains plead his cause; that, if the complaints of the Locrians were founded in truth, he should be put to death in prison, and his effects confiscated. That Publius Scipio should be recalled for having quitted his province without the permission of the Senate."

A hot debate followed, in which, "besides the atrocious conduct of Pleminius, much was said about the dress of the general himself, as being not only un-Roman, but even un-soldierly." His critics complained that "he

walked about the gymnasium in a cloak and
slippers, and that he gave his whole time to light
books and the palæstra. That his whole staff
were enjoying the delights which Syracuse
afforded, with the same indolence and effeminacy.
That Carthage and Hannibal had dropped out
of his memory "—somewhat inconsistent on the
part of the people who were proposing to recall
him because he had been fighting with Hannibal.
How petty, but how true to human nature!
The real grievance of his crusted seniors was not
his leniency with Pleminius, but his Greek
refinement and studies.

But wiser counsels prevailed. Metellus pointed
out how inconsistent it would be for the State
now to recall, condemned in his absence and
without a hearing, the very man whom they
had commissioned to finish the war, and to do
so in the face of the Locrians' evidence that
none of their tribulations occurred while Scipio
was there. On the motion of Metellus a commission of inquiry was appointed to visit Scipio
in Sicily, or even in Africa had he departed
thither, with power to deprive him of his command if they found that the acts at Locri had
been committed at his command or with his
concurrence. This commission was also to investigate the charges brought against his military
régime, whether his own alleged indolency or

the relaxation of discipline among the troops. These charges were brought by Cato, who, besides being an adherent of Fabius, conceived it his special mission in life to oppose the new Hellenic culture and to effect cheese-paring economies. It is related that to save money he sold his slaves as soon as they were too old for work, that he esteemed his wife no more than his slaves, and that he left behind in Spain his faithful charger rather than incur the charge of transporting it to Italy. As quæstor under Scipio in Sicily he reproached his general with his liberality to the troops, until Scipio dispensed with his services, whereupon Cato returned disgruntled to Italy to join Fabius in an anti-waste campaign in the Senate.

The commission went first to Locri. Pleminius had already been thrown into prison at Rhegium, according to some accounts by Scipio, who had sent a *legatus* with a guard to seize him and his principal coadjutors. At Locri restitution of their property and civic privileges was made to the citizens, and they willingly agreed to send deputies to give evidence against Pleminius at Rome. But though invited to bring complaints against Scipio, the citizens declined, saying that they were convinced that the injuries inflicted on them were neither by his orders nor with his approval.

The commission, relieved of the duty of investigating such charges, nevertheless went on to Syracuse, to see for themselves the military condition of his command.   There are parallels in history to such a political investigation on the eve of a great military venture—the Nivelle affair is the most recent,—and often they have reacted disastrously both on the confidence of the commander and the confidence of his subordinates in him.   But Scipio survived the test. "While they were on their way to Syracuse, Scipio prepared to clear himself, not by words but by facts.   He ordered all his troops to assemble there, and the fleet to be got in readiness, as though a battle had to be fought that day with the Carthaginians by sea and land.   On the day of their arrival he entertained them hospitably, and on the next day presented to their view his land and sea forces, not only drawn up in order, but the former carrying out field operations, while the fleet fought a mock naval battle in the harbour.   The prætor and the deputies were then conducted round to view the armouries, the granaries, and other preparations for the war. And so great was the admiration aroused in them of each particular, and the whole together, that they formed the conviction that under the conduct of that general, and with that army, the Carthaginians would be vanquished, or by none other. They bid him with the blessing of the gods, cross over. . . . " (Livy).

These deputies were not, as the "frocks" of 1914-18, remarkable only for their ignorance of matters military. Like most Romans they were men of military training and experience, and no "eye-wash" would have deceived them. In face of such a verdict it is surprising that a historian of the reputation of Mommsen should here again swallow Fabius's spiteful charges, and repeat as his own the opinion that Scipio failed to maintain discipline. Only a lay historian, militarily ignorant, could imagine that an army which had been allowed to run to seed could carry out the complex Roman battle drill and develop its preparations to a pitch of efficiency that not only gained the approval but aroused the enthusiasm of this expert commission.

On their return to Rome the warmth of their praise induced the Senate to vote that Scipio should cross to Africa, and that he should be given permission to select himself, *out of those forces which were in Sicily*, the troops which he wanted to accompany him. The irony of this grudging and tardy permission lies in the clause in italics. He was given their blessing, and that was all. For a venture of such magnitude, he was worse supported by the Senate than even Hannibal by Carthage. Of Roman troops, apart

from his own volunteers, he had in Sicily only
the 5th and 6th Legions, the remnant of those
who had fought at Cannæ, and who in punishment for the defeat had been sentenced to serve
in exile in Sicily. A less understanding commander might well have hesitated to rely on troops
suffering such a degradation. But "Scipio was
very far from feeling contempt for such soldiers,
inasmuch as he knew that the defeat at Cannæ
was not attributable to their cowardice, and
that there were no soldiers in the Roman army
who had served so long, or were so experienced
in the various types of combat." They on
their side were burning to wipe off the unjust
stigma of disgrace, and when he declared that
he would take them with him he could feel
sure that by this proof of his trust and generosity
he had won their utter devotion. He inspected
them "man by man," and putting aside those
unfit for service he filled up their places with
his own men, bringing the strength of each
Legion up to 6200 infantry and 300 horse.

Roman accounts differ widely as to the total
strength of the force that embarked, and even
in Livy's time the uncertainty was such that he
preferred not to give an opinion. The smallest
estimate is 10,000 foot and 200 horse; a second
is 16,000 infantry and 1600 horse; the third,
and largest, is a total of 35,000, including horse

and foot. The first is disproved by the previous facts, and these seem rather to point to the second as the correct estimate. In any case it was slender indeed for the object aimed at.

There is a striking parallel between the situation and numbers of Scipio in 204 B.C. and those of Gustavus Adolphus in 1630 A.D., when the Swedish King crossed the Baltic to strike at the seat of the Imperial power. And each force, small as it was, had been welded by the training genius and personal magnetism of its leader into a superb instrument of war—a cadre or framework for later expansion. How purely this expedition and its triumphant success was the plan and the work of Scipio can be aptly shown by quoting Mommsen, a far from friendly witness : " It was evident that the Senate did not appoint the expedition, but merely allowed it : Scipio did not obtain half the resources which had formerly been placed at the command of Regulus, and he got that very corps which for years had been subjected by the Senate to intentional degradation. The African army was, in the view of the majority of the Senate, a forlorn hope of disrated companies and volunteers, whose loss in any event the State had no great occasion to regret." And yet many historians assert that Rome's victory in the Punic War was due to the generous support she gave to her generals, the failure of Carthage to the reverse cause !

Not only were Scipio's means slender, but the African situation had changed for the worse during the year's delay forced on him by the need to raise and train his expeditionary force, in default of Rome's aid, a delay still further protracted by the Locri inquiry.   Hasdrubal, son of Gisco, on his return from Spain had check-mated Scipio's newly won influence over Syphax, by giving the king his daughter Sophonisba in marriage, and in return got Syphax to renew his pledge of alliance with Carthage.   Still afraid that Syphax would adhere to his old pledges to Scipio, Hasdrubal "took advantage of the Nu-midian while under the influence of the first transports of love, and calling to his aid the caresses of the bride, prevailed upon him to send envoys into Sicily to Scipio, and by them to warn him 'not to cross over into Africa in reliance on his former promise.' "   The message begged Scipio to carry on the war elsewhere, so that Syphax might maintain his neutrality, adding that if the Romans came he would be com-pelled to fight against them.

Passion had beaten diplomacy.   One can im-agine what a blow the message proved to Scipio. Yet he determined to carry through his plan, and merely sought to counteract the moral harm which might accrue if Syphax's defection became known. He sent the envoys back as quickly as possible, with a stern reminder to Syphax of his treaty obligations. Further, realising that the envoys had been seen by many, and that if he maintained silence about their visit rumours would spread, Scipio announced to the troops that the envoys had come, like Masinissa earlier to Lælius, to urge him to hasten his invasion of Africa. It was a shrewd ruse, for the truth might have caused grave moral depression at the critical time. Scipio, wiser than the military authorities of 1914, understood crowd psychology, and knew that the led put the worst construction on the silence of the leaders, that they assume no news to be bad news, despite all the proverbs.

CHAPTER IX.

AFRICA.

THUS in the spring of 204 B.C. Scipio embarked his army at Lilybæum (modern Marsala), and sailed for Africa. His fleet is said to have comprised forty warships and four hundred transports, and on board was carried water and rations for fifty-five days, of which fifteen days' supply was cooked. Complete dispositions were made for the protection of the convoy by the warships, and each class of vessel was distinguished by lights at night—the transports one, the warships two, and his own flagship three. It is worth notice that he personally supervised the embarkation of the troops.

A huge crowd gathered to witness the departure, not only the inhabitants of Lilybæum, but all the deputies from Sicily—as a compliment to Scipio,—and the troops who were being left behind. At daybreak Scipio delivered a farewell oration and prayer, and then by a trumpet gave the signal to weigh anchor. Favoured by a strong wind the fleet made a quick passage, and next morning when the sun rose they were in sight of land, and could discern the promontory of Mercury (now Cape Bon). Scipio ordered the pilot to make for a landing farther west, but a dense fog coming on later forced the fleet to cast anchor. Next morning, the wind rising, dispelled the fog, and the army disembarked at the Fair promontory (now Cape Farina), a few miles from the important city of Utica. The security of the landing was at once ensured by entrenching a camp on the nearest rising ground.

These two promontories formed the horns, pointing towards Sicily, of the territory of Carthage, that bull's head of land projecting into the Mediterranean which is to-day known as Tunisia. The horns, some thirty-five miles apart, enclosed a vast semicircular bay in the centre of which stood Carthage, on a small peninsula pointing east. Utica lay just below and inside the tip of the western horn, and a few miles east of the city was the Bagradas river, whose rich and fertile valley was the main source of supplies for Carthage. Another strategic point was Tunis, at the junction of the Carthage peninsula with the mainland—geographically south-west of Carthage but militarily east, because it lay across the landward approaches from that flank.

Although the Carthaginians had long been

expecting the blow, and had watch-towers on every cape, the news created feverish excitement and alarm, stimulated by the stream of fugitives from the country districts. At Carthage, emergency defensive measures were taken as if Scipio was already at the gates. The Roman's first step was clearly to gain a secure base of operations, and with this aim his preliminary move was against Utica. His fleet was despatched there forthwith while the army marched overland, his advanced guard cavalry encountering a body of five hundred Carthaginian horse who had been sent to reconnoitre and interrupt the landing. After a sharp engagement these were put to flight. A still better omen was the arrival of Masinissa, true to his word, to join Scipio. Livy states that the earlier sources from which he compiled his history differed as to the strength of Masinissa's reinforcement, some saying that he brought two hundred horse, and some two thousand. Livy accepts the smaller estimate, for the very sound reason that Masinissa after his return from Spain had been driven out of his father's kingdom by the joint efforts of Syphax and the Carthaginians, and for the past year and more had been eluding pursuit by repeated changes of quarter. An exile, who had escaped from the last battle with only sixty horsemen, it is unlikely that he could have raised his band of followers to any large proportions.

Meanwhile, the Carthaginians despatched a further body of four thousand horse, mainly Numidians, to oppose Scipio's advance and gain time for Syphax and Hasdrubal to come to their aid. To their ally and to their chief general in Africa the most urgent messages had been sent. Hanno with the four thousand cavalry occupied a town, Salæca, about fifteen miles from the Roman camp near Utica, and it is said by Livy that Scipio, on hearing of this, remarked, " What, cavalry lodging in houses during the summer ! Let there be even more in number while they have such a leader." " Concluding that the more dilatory they were in their operations, the more active he ought to be, he sent Masinissa forward with the cavalry, directing him to ride up to the gates of the enemy and draw them out to battle, and when their whole force had poured out and committed themselves thoroughly to the attack, then to retire by degrees." Scipio himself waited for what he judged sufficient time for Masinissa's advanced party to draw out the enemy, and then followed with the Roman cavalry, " proceeding without being seen, under cover of some rising ground." He took up a position near the so-called Tower of Agathocles, on the northern slope of a saddle between two ridges.

BRITISH MILES

0   1   2

UTICA

ANCIENT

COAST LINE

SCIPIO'S CAMP

SCIPIO'S CAMP

CASTRA CORNELIA

SCIPIO

HANNO

MASINISSA

DJEBEL MENZEL ROUL

UTICA

TO ILLUSTRATE

(A) *SCIPIO'S AMBUSH OF HANNO.*
(B) *SCIPIO'S SURPRISE ATTACK ON THE CAMPS OF HASDRUBAL & SYPHAX*

LAELIUS

SCIPIO

MASINISSA

SYPHAX'S CAMP

HASDRUBAL'S CAMP

KOUDIAT TOUBA

BASED ON KROMAYER-VEITH.

Masinissa, following Scipio's plan, made repeated advances and retirements. At first he
drew out small skirmishing parties, then counter-
attacked them so that Hanno was forced to reinforce them, lured them on again by a simulated
retreat and repeated the process. At last Hanno,
irritated by these tactical tricks—so typical of
the Parthians and the Mongols later,—sallied
forth with his main body, whereupon Masinissa
retired slowly, drawing the Carthaginians along
the southern side of the ridges and past the
saddle which concealed the Roman cavalry.
When the moment was ripe, Scipio's cavalry
emerged and encircled the flank and rear of
Hanno's cavalry, while Masinissa, turning about,
attacked them in front. The first line of a
thousand were surrounded and slain, and of the
remainder two thousand were captured or killed
in a vigorous pursuit.

Scipio followed up this success by a seven days'
circuit through the countryside, clearing it of
cattle and supplies, and creating a wide devas-
tated zone as a barrier against attack. Security,
both in supply and protection, thus effected, he
concentrated his efforts on the siege of Utica,
which he wanted for his base of operations.
Utica, however, was not destined to be a second
Cartagena. Although he combined attack from
the sea by the marines with the land as-

sault, the fortress defied all his efforts and ruses.

Hasdrubal by this time had collected a force of thirty thousand foot and three thousand horse, but with painful recollections of the maulings he had suffered in Spain, did not venture to move to Utica's relief until reinforced by Syphax. When the latter at last came, with an army stated to have been fifty thousand foot and ten thousand horse, the menace compelled Scipio to raise the siege—after forty days. Faced with such a concentration of hostile force, Scipio's situation must have been hazardous, but he extricated himself without mishap and fortified a camp for the winter on a small peninsula, connected to the mainland by a narrow isthmus. This lay on the eastern, or Carthage, side of Utica, thus lying on the flank of any relieving force, and was later known as Castra Cornelia. The enemy then encamped some seven miles farther east, covering the approaches to the River Bagradas.

If there is a parallel between Scipio's landing in Africa and Gustavus's landing in Germany, there is a still more striking parallel between their action during the first season on hostile soil. Both campaigns to the unmilitary critic appear limited in scope compared with the avowed object with which they had set forth. Both generals have been criticised for over-caution, if not hesitation. And both were justified not only by the result, but by the science of war. Scipio and Gustavus alike, unable for reasons outside their control to adjust the means to the end, displayed that rare strategical quality—of adjusting the end to the means. Their strategy foreshadowed Napoleon's maxim that " the whole art of war consists in a well ordered and prudent defensive, followed by a bold and rapid offensive." Both sought first to lay the foundations for the offensive which followed by gaining a secure base of operations where they could build up their means to a strength adequate to ensure the attainment of the end.

Gustavus is known to have been a great student of the classics : was his strategy in 1630 perhaps a conscious application of Scipio's method ? Nor is this campaign of Gustavus's the only military parallel with Scipio's that history records. For the action of Wellington in fortifying and retiring behind the lines of Torres Vedras in 1810 to checkmate the French superior concentration of force has a vivid reminder, both topographical and strategical, of Scipio's action in face of the concentration of Syphax and Hasdrubal.

In this secure retreat Scipio devoted the winter to build up his strength and supplies for the next spring's campaign. Besides the corn he had collected in his preliminary foraging march, he obtained a vast quantity from Sardinia, and also fresh stores of clothing and arms from Sicily. The success of his landing, his sharp punishment of the Carthaginian attempts to meet him in battle, and, above all, the fact that he had dissipated the terrors of the unknown, had falsified all the fears of the wiseacres, by holding his own, small though his force, on the dreaded soil of Africa, almost at the gates of Carthage—all these factors combined to turn the current of opinion and arouse the State to give him adequate support. Reliefs were sent to Sicily so that he could reinforce his strength with the troops at first left behind for local defence.

But, as usual, while seeking to develop his own strength, he did not overlook the value of subtracting from the enemy's. He reopened negotiations with Syphax, "whose passion for his bride he thought might now perhaps have become satiated from unlimited enjoyment." In these he was disappointed, for while Syphax went so far as to suggest terms of peace by which the Carthaginians should quit Italy in return for a Roman evacuation of Africa, he did not hold out any hope that he would abandon the Carthaginian cause if the war continued.

For such terms Scipio had no use, but he only rejected them in a qualified manner, in order to maintain a pretext for his emissaries to visit the hostile camp. The reason was that he had conceived a plan whereby to weaken the enemy and anticipate the attack that he feared owing to the enemy's heavy superiority of numbers. Some of his earlier messengers to Syphax had reported that the Carthaginians' winter huts were built almost entirely of wood, and those of the Numidians of interwoven reeds and matting, disposed without order or proper intervals, and that a number even lay outside the ramparts of the camps. This news suggested to Scipio the idea of setting fire to the enemy's camp and striking a surprise blow in the confusion.

Therefore in his later embassies Scipio sent certain expert scouts and picked centurions dressed as officers' servants. While the conferences were in progress, these rambled through the camps, both that of Syphax and of Hasdrubal, noting their approaches and entrances and studying the general plan of the camps, the distance between them, the times and methods of stationing guards and outposts. With each embassy, too, a different lot of observers were sent, so that as large a number as possible should familiarise themselves with the lie of the enemy camps. As a result of their reports Scipio ascertained that Syphax's camp was the more inflammable and the easier to attack.

He then sent further envoys to Syphax, who was hoping for peace, with instructions not to return until they received a decisive answer on the proposed terms, saying that it was time that either an agreement was settled or the war vigorously prosecuted. After consultation between Syphax and Hasdrubal, they apparently decided to accept, whereupon Scipio made further stipulations, as a suitable way of terminating the truce, which he did next day, informing Syphax that while he himself desired peace, the rest of his council were opposed to it. By this means he gained freedom to carry out his plan without breaking his faith, though he undoubtedly went as close to the border between strategical ruse and deliberate craft as was possible without overstepping it.

Syphax, much vexed at this breakdown of negotiations, at once conferred with Hasdrubal, and it was decided to take the offensive and challenge Scipio to battle, on level ground if possible. But Scipio was ready to strike, his preparations complete. Even in his final preparations, he sought to mystify and mislead the enemy in order to make his surprise more effective. The orders issued to the troops spoke of the surprise being aimed at Utica ; he launched his ships and mounted on board siege machines as if he was about to assault Utica from the sea, and he despatched two thousand infantry to seize a hill which commanded the town. This move had a dual purpose—to convince the enemy that his plan was directed against Utica, and to occupy the city garrison to prevent them making a sortie against his camp when he marched out to attack the hostile camps. Thus he was able to achieve economy of force, by concentrating the bulk of his troops for the decisive blow, and leaving only a slight force to guard the camp, and thus once more he did not lose sight of the principle of security in carrying out that of surprise. He had fixed the enemy's attention in the wrong direction.

About mid-day he summoned a conference of his ablest and most trusted tribunes and disclosed his plan. To this conference he summoned the officers who had been to the enemy's camp. "He questioned them closely and compared the accounts they gave of the approaches and entrances of the camp, letting Masinissa decide, and following his advice owing to his personal knowledge of the ground." Then he ordered the tribunes to give the troops their evening meal early, and lead the legions out of the camp after "Retreat" had been sounded as usual. On this point Polybius adds the interesting note

that " it is the custom among the Romans at
supper-time for the trumpeters to sound their
instruments outside the general's tent as a signal
that it is time to set the night-watches at their
several posts."

About the first watch the troops were formed
up in march order and moved off on their seven-
mile march, and about midnight arrived in the
vicinity of the hostile camps, which were just
over a mile apart. Thereupon Scipio divided his
force, placing all the Numidians and half his
legionaries under Lælius and Masinissa with
orders to attack Syphax's camp. The two commanders he first took aside and urged on them
the need for caution, emphasising that " the more
the darkness in night attacks hinders and im-
pedes the sight, the more must one supply the
place of actual vision by skill and care." He
further instructed them that he would wait to
launch his attack on Hasdrubal's camp until
Lælius had set fire to the other camp, and with
this purpose marched his own men at a slow
pace.

Lælius and Masinissa, dividing their force,
attacked the camp from two directions simultaneously—a convergent manœuvre,—and Masinissa also posted his Numidians, because of their
knowledge of the camp, to cut off the various
exits of escape. As had been foreseen, once the

leading Romans had set the fire alight, it spread rapidly along the first row of huts, and in a brief while the whole camp was aflame, because of the closeness of the huts and the lack of proper intervals between rows.

Fully imagining that it was an accidental conflagration, Syphax's men rushed out of their huts unarmed, and in a disorderly flight. Many perished in their huts while half asleep, many were trampled to death in the frenzied rush for the exits, while those who escaped the flames were cut down unawares by the Numidians posted at the gates of the camp.

Meanwhile in the Carthaginian camp the soldiers, aroused by the sentries' report of the fire in the other camp, and seeing how vast was the volume of flame, rushed out of their own camp to assist in extinguishing the fire, they also imagining it an accident and Scipio seven miles distant. This was as Scipio had hoped and anticipated, and he at once fell on the rabble, giving orders not to let a man escape to give warning to the troops still in the camp. Instantly he followed up this by launching his attack on the gates of the camp, which were unguarded as a result of the confusion.

By the cleverness of his plan in attacking Syphax's camp first, he had turned to advantage the fact that a number of the latter's huts were

outside the ramparts and so easily accessible,
and had created the opportunity to force the
gates of the better protected Carthaginian camp.

The first troops inside set fire to the nearest
huts, and soon the whole camp was aflame, the
same scenes of confusion and destruction being
here repeated, and those who escaped through
the gates meeting their fate at the hands of
Roman parties posted for the purpose. " Hasdrubal at once desisted from any attempt to
extinguish the fire, as he knew now from what
had befallen him that the calamity which had
overtaken the Numidians also was not, as they
had supposed, the result of chance, but was due
to the initiative and daring of the enemy."
He therefore forced his way out and escaped,
along with only two thousand foot and five
hundred horsemen, half-armed and many wounded
or scorched. With this small force he took refuge
in a near-by town, but when Scipio's pursuing
troops came up, and seeing that the inhabitants
were disaffected, he resumed his flight to Carthage. Syphax who had also escaped, probably
with a larger proportion, retired to a fortified
position at Abba, a town quite close.

The armies of Sennacherib had not suffered
a swifter, more unexpected, or more complete
fate than those of Hasdrubal and Syphax.
According to Livy forty thousand men were

either slain or destroyed by the flames, and about five thousand were captured, including many Carthaginian nobles. As a spectacle of disaster it surpasses any in history. Polybius, who presumably got his information from Lælius and other eye-witnesses, thus describes it : "The whole place was filled with wailing and confused cries, panic, fear, strange noises, and above all raging fire and flames that overbore all resistance, things any one of which would be sufficient to strike terror into a human heart, and how much more this extraordinary combination of them all. It is not possible to find any other disaster which however magnified could be compared with this, so much did it exceed in horror all previous events. Therefore of all the brilliant exploits performed by Scipio this seems to me the most brilliant and most adventurous. . . ."

In Carthage the news caused great alarm and anxiety—Hasdrubal's purpose in retreating there had been to allay the panic and forestall any capitulation. His presence and his resolute spirit was needed. The Carthaginians had expected with the spring campaign to find their armies shutting in Scipio on the cape near Utica, cutting him off by land and sea. Finding the tables so dramatically turned, they swung from confidence to extreme despondency. At an emergency debate in the Senate three different opinions were put forward: to send envoys to Scipio to treat for peace; to recall Hannibal; to raise fresh levies and urge Syphax to renew the struggle in co-operation with them. The influence of Hasdrubal, combined with that of all the Barcine party, carried the day, and the last policy was adopted. It is worth a passing note, in view of the charge of ultra-Roman prejudice often made against Livy, that he speaks with obvious admiration of this third motion which " breathed the spirit of Roman constancy and adversity."

Syphax and his Numidians had at first decided to continue their retreat and, abandoning the war, retire to their own country, but three influences caused them to change their minds. These were the pleadings of Sophonisba to Syphax not to desert her father and his people, the prompt arrival of the envoys from Carthage, and the arrival of a body of over four thousand Celtiberian mercenaries from Spain — whose numbers were exaggerated by popular rumour, doubtless inspired by the war party, to ten thousand. Accordingly Syphax gave the envoys a message that he would co-operate with Hasdrubal, and showed them the first reinforcement of fresh Numidian levies who had arrived. By energetic recruiting Hasdrubal and Syphax were able to take the field again within thirty days, joining forces, and entrenched a camp on the Great Plain. Their strength is put as between thirty and thirty-five thousand fighting men.

Scipio, after his dispersion of the enemy's field forces in the recent surprise, had turned his attention to the siege of Utica, in order to gain the secure base which he wanted as a prelude to further operations. It is evident that he intentionally refrained from pressing the retreat of Syphax, for such pressure by forcing the latter to fight would tend to pour fresh fuel on a fire that was flickering out of itself. The ground for such a hope we have already shown, as also the factors which caused its disappointment. Polybius gives us a valuable sidelight at this juncture on Scipio's care and forethought for his troops—" He also at the same time distributed the booty, but expelled the merchants who were making too good an affair of it ; for as their recent success had made them form a rosy picture of the future, the soldiers attached no value to their actual booty, and were very ready to dispose of it for a song to the merchants."

When the news reached Scipio of the junction of the Carthaginian and Numidian forces and of their approach, he acted promptly. Leaving only a small detachment to keep up the appearance of a siege by land and sea, he set out to meet the enemy, his whole force being in light marching order—he evidently judged that rapidity was the key to this fresh menace, to strike before they could weld their new force into a strong weapon. On the fifth day he reached the Great Plain, and fortified a camp on a hill some three and a half miles distant from the enemy's camp. The two following days he advanced his forces, harassing the enemy's outposts, in order to tempt them out to battle. The bait succeeded on the third day, and the enemy's combined army came out of their camp and drew up in order of battle. They placed the Celtiberians, their picked troops, in the centre, the Numidians on the left, and the Carthaginians on the right. " Scipio simply followed the usual Roman practice of placing the maniples of *hastati* in front, behind them the *principes*, and hindmost of all the *triarii*." He disposed his Italian cavalry on his right, facing Syphax's Numidians, and Masinissa's Numidians on his left, facing the Carthaginian horse. At the first encounter the enemy's wings were broken by the Italian and Masinissa's cavalry. Scipio's rapidity of march and foresight in striking before Hasdrubal and Syphax had consolidated their raw levies was abundantly justified. Moreover, on one side moral was heightened by recent success, and on the other lowered by recent disaster.

In the centre the Celtiberians fought staunchly, knowing that flight was useless, because of their ignorance of the country, and that surrender was futile, because of their treason in coming from Spain to take service against the Romans. It would appear that Scipio used his second and third lines—the *principes* and *triarii*—as a mobile reserve to attack the Celtiberians' flanks, instead of to reinforce the *hastati* directly, as was the normal custom. Thus surrounded on all sides the Celtiberians were cut to pieces where they stood, though only after an obstinate resistance, which enabled the commanders, Hasdrubal and Syphax, as well as a good number of the fugitives, to make their escape. Hasdrubal with his Carthaginian survivors found shelter in Carthage, and Syphax with his cavalry retreated home to his own capital, Cirta.

Night had put a stop to the scene of carnage, and next day Scipio sent Masinissa and Lælius in pursuit of Syphax, while he himself cleared the surrounding country, and occupied its strong places, as a preliminary to a move on Carthage. Here fresh alarm had been caused, but the people were more staunch in the hour of trial than is the tendency to regard them. Few voices were raised in favour of peace, and energetic measures were taken for resistance. The city was provisioned for a long siege, and the work of strengthening and enlarging the fortifications was pushed on. At the same time the Senate decided to send the fleet to attack the Roman ships at Utica and attempt to raise the siege, and as a further step the recall of Hannibal was decided on.

Scipio, lightening his transport by the despatch of the booty to his camp near Utica, had already reached and occupied Tunis, with little opposition despite the strength of the place. Tunis was only some fifteen miles from Carthage and could be clearly seen, and as Polybius tells us of Scipio, " this he thought would be a most effective means of striking the Carthaginians with terror and dismay "—the moral objective again.

Hardly had he completed this " bound," however, before his sentries sighted the Carthaginian fleet sailing past the place. He realised what their plan was and also the danger, knowing that his own ships, burdened with siege machines or converted into transports, were unprepared for a naval battle. Unhesitatingly, he made his decision to stave off the threat, and made a forced march back to Utica. There was no time to clear his ships for action, and so he hit on the plan of anchoring the warships close inshore, and protecting them by a four-deep row of transports lashed together as a floating wall.

He also laid planks from one to the other, to
enable the free movement of troops, leaving
narrow intervals for small patrol-boats to pass
in and out under these bridges. He then put
on board the transports a thousand picked men
with a very high proportion of weapons, particularly missiles—an interesting point in fore-
shadowing the modern doctrine of using increased
fire-power in defence to replace man-power.

These emergency measures were completed
before the enemy's attack came, thanks first
to the slow sailing of the Carthaginian fleet,
and their further delay in offering battle in the
open sea. Thus they were forced to sail in
against the Romans' unexpected type of formation, like ships attacking a wall. Their weight
of numbers, too, was partly discounted by the
fact of the transports being higher out of the
water, so that the Carthaginians had to throw
their weapons upwards, and the Romans, con-
versely, gained additional impetus and better
aim through casting their missiles from a superior
height. But the device of sending patrol-boats
and light craft out through the intervals to
harass the Carthaginian ships—a device obviously
adapted by Scipio from military tactics—failed
of its effect, and proved an actual handicap to
the defence. For when they went out to harass
the approaching warships they were run down

by the mere momentum and bulk of the latter, and in the later stages became so intermingled with the Carthaginian ships as to mask the fire of the troops on the transports.

Beaten off in their direct assaults, the Carthaginians tried a new measure, throwing long beams with iron hooks at the end on to the Roman transports, these beams being secured by chains to their own vessels. By this means the fastenings were broken, and a number of transports dragged away, the troops manning them having barely time to leap on to the second line of ships. Only one line had been broken, and the opposition had been so severe that the Carthaginians contented themselves with this limited success, and sailed back to Carthage. They towed away six captured transports, though doubtless more were broken adrift and lost by the Romans.

Baulked in this quarter, the Carthaginians' hopes were shattered in another, for the pursuing force sent by Scipio after Syphax had fulfilled its object and finally cut away this prop of Carthaginian power in Africa. The success went still further, as it gained for Scipio that Numidian source of man-power which he had so long schemed for, and which he needed to build up his forces to an adequate strength for his decisive blow.

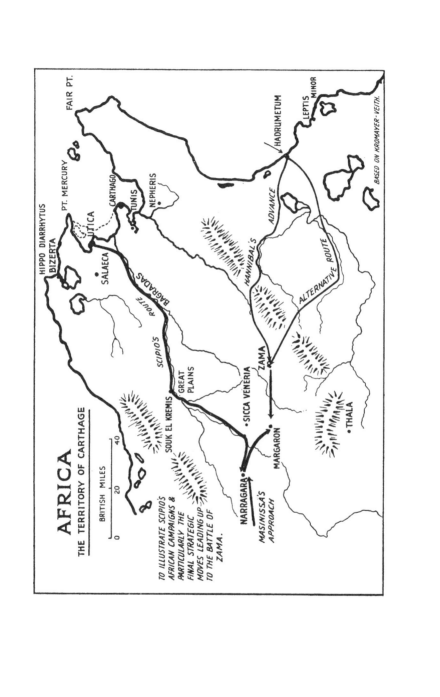

AFRICA
THE TERRITORY OF CARTHAGE

BRITISH MILES

0   20   40

TO ILLUSTRATE SCIPIO'S
AFRICAN CAMPAIGNS &
PARTICULARLY THE
FINAL STRATEGIC
MOVES LEADING UP
TO THE BATTLE OF
ZAMA.

FAIR PT.

PT. MERCURY

HIPPO DIARRHYTUS
BIZERTA

CARTHAGO
TUNIS
UTICA
NEPHERIS

SALAECA

SCIPIO'S ROUTE

BAGRADAS

GREAT PLAINS

SOUK EL KREMIS

SICCA VENERIA

ZAMA

HANNIBAL'S ADVANCE

HADRUMETUM

LEPTIS MINOR

ALTERNATIVE ROUTE

THALA

MARGARON

NARRAGARA

MASINISSA'S APPROACH

BASED ON KROMAYER-VEITH.

Following up Syphax, Lælius and Masinissa arrived in Massylia (Masinissa's hereditary kingdom from which he had been driven) after a fifteen days' march, and there expelled the garrisons left by Syphax. The latter had fallen back farther east to his own dominions, Massæsylia—modern Algeria,—and there, spurred on by his wife, raised a fresh force from the abundant resources of his kingdom. He proceeded to organise them on the Roman model, imagining, like so many military copyists in history, that imitation of externals gave him the secret of the Roman success. His force was large enough— as large, in fact, as his original strength,—but it was utterly raw and undisciplined. With this he advanced to meet Lælius and Masinissa. At the first encounter between the opposing cavalry, numerical superiority told, but the advantage was lost when the Roman infantry reinforced the intervals of their cavalry, and before long the raw troops broke and fled. The victory was essentially one due to superior training and discipline, and not to any subtle manœuvre such as appears in all Scipio's battles. This is worth note in view of the fact that some historians lose no opportunity of hinting that Scipio's success was due more to his able lieutenants than to himself.

Syphax, seeing his force crumbling, sought to

shame his men into resistance by riding forward
and exposing himself to danger. In this gallant
attempt he was unhorsed, made prisoner, and
dragged into the presence of Lælius. As Livy
remarks, this was " a spectacle calculated to
afford peculiar satisfaction to Masinissa." The
latter showed fine military spirit as well as
judgment after the battle, when he declared to
Lælius that, much as he would like to visit his
regained kingdom, " it was not proper in prosperity any more than in adversity to lose time."
He therefore asked permission to push on with
the cavalry to Cirta, Syphax's capital, while
Lælius followed with the infantry. Having won
Lælius's assent, Masinissa advanced, taking
Syphax with him. On arrival in front of Cirta,
he summoned the principal inhabitants to appear,
but they refused until he showed them Syphax
in chains, whereupon the faint-hearted threw open
the gates. Masinissa, posting guards, galloped
off to seize the palace, and was met by Sophonisba.
This woman, almost as famous as Helen or
Cleopatra for her beauty and for her disastrous
influence, made such a clever appeal to his
pride, his pity, and his passion, that she not
only won his pledge not to hand her over to the
Romans, but " as the Numidians are an exces-
sively amorous race, he became the slave of his
captive." When she had withdrawn, and he had

to face the problem of how to reconcile his duty with his pledge, his passion suggested to him a loophole—to marry her himself that very day. When Lælius came up he was so annoyed that at first he was on the point of having her dragged from the marriage-bed and sent with the other captives to the Utica camp, but afterwards relented, agreeing to leave the decision to Scipio. The two then set to work on the reduction of the remaining towns in Numidia, which were still garrisoned by the troops of Syphax.

When the captives arrived at Scipio's camp, Syphax himself in chains at their head, the troops poured out to see the spectacle. What a contrast with a few years back! Now, a captive in chains; then, a powerful ruler who held the balance of power, for whose friendship Scipio and Hasdrubal vied on their simultaneous visits, both placing themselves in his power, so highly did they assess the prize at stake.

This thought evidently passed through Scipio's mind, the recollection, too, of their quondam friendship, and moved him to sympathy. He questioned Syphax as to the motives that had led him to break his pledge of alliance with the Romans and make war on them unprovoked. Syphax, gaining confidence from Scipio's manner, replied that he had been mad to do so, but that taking up arms was only the consummation of his frenzy, and not its beginning, which dated from his marriage to Sophonisba. " That fury and pest " had fascinated and blinded him to his undoing. But ruined and fallen as he was, he declared that he gained some consolation from seeing her fatal lures transferred to his greatest enemy.

These words caused Scipio great anxiety, for he appreciated both her influence and the menace to the Roman plans from Masinissa's hasty wedding. She had detached one passionate Numidian; she might well lead astray another. When Lælius and Masinissa arrived shortly after, Scipio showed no signs of his feelings in his public greeting, praising both in the highest terms for their work. But as soon as possible he took Masinissa aside privately. His talk with the delinquent was a masterpiece of tact and psychological appeal. " I suppose, Masinissa, that it was because you saw in me some good qualities that you first came to me when in Spain for the purpose of forming a friendship with me, and that afterwards in Africa you committed yourself and all your hopes to my protection. But of all those virtues, which made me seem worthy of your regard, there is none of which I am so proud as temperance and control of my passions." Then pointing out the dangers caused by want of self-control,

he continued : " I have mentioned with delight,
and I remember with pleasure, the instances of
fortitude and courage you displayed in my
absence. As to other matters, I would rather
that you should reflect on them in private,
than that I should cause you to blush by reciting
them." Then, with a final call to Masinissa's
sense of duty, he dismissed him. Where reproaches might have stiffened Masinissa, such
a friendly appeal broke him down, and bursting
into tears, he retired to his own tent. Here,
after a prolonged inward struggle, he sent for a
confidential servant, and ordered him to mix
some poison in a cup and carry it to Sophonisba,
with the message that "Masinissa would gladly
have fulfilled the first obligation which as a
husband he owed to her, his wife ; but as those
who had the power had deprived him of the
exercise of those rights, he now performed his
second promise—that she should not come alive
into the power of the Romans." When the
servant came to Sophonisba she said, " I accept
this nuptial present ; nor is it an unwelcome
one, if my husband can render me no better
service. Tell him, however, that I should have
died with greater satisfaction had I not married
so near on my death." Then, calmly and without
a quiver, she took and drained the cup.

As soon as Scipio heard the news, fearing that

the high-spirited young man, when so distraught, might take some desperate step, " he immediately sent for him, and at one time endeavoured to solace him, at another gently rebuked him for trying to expiate one rash act with another, and making the affair more tragical than was necessary."

Next day Scipio sought to erase this grief from Masinissa's mind by a well-calculated appeal to his ambition and pride. Summoning an assembly, he first saluted Masinissa by the title of king, speaking in the highest terms of his achievements, and then presented him with a golden goblet, an ivory sceptre, a curule chair, and other symbols of honour. " He increased the honour by observing that among the Romans there was nothing more magnificent than a ' triumph,' and that those who received the reward of a ' triumph ' were not invested with more splendid ornaments than those of which the Roman people considered Masinissa alone, of all foreigners, worthy." This action, and the encouragement to his dreams of becoming master of all Numidia, had the desired effect, and Masinissa speedily forgot his private sorrows in his public distinction. Lælius, whom Scipio had been careful to praise similarly and reward, was then sent with Syphax and the other captives back to Rome.

CHAPTER X.

A VIOLATED PEACE.

HIS political base in Africa secured, Scipio
moved back to Tunis, and this time the moral
threat, strengthened by recent events, was successful. It tilted the scales against the war party,
and the Carthaginians sent thirty of their principal elders—the Council of Elders being superior
even to the Senate—to beg for terms of peace.
According to Livy, they prostrated themselves
in Eastern manner on entering Scipio's presence,
and their pleas showed equal humility. They
implored pardon for their State, saying that it
had been twice brought to the brink of ruin
by the rashness of its citizens, and they hoped
it would again owe its safety to the indulgence
of its enemies. This hope was based on their
knowledge that the Roman people's aim was
dominion, and not destruction, and they declared
that they would accept whatever terms he saw
fit to grant. Scipio replied " that he had come
to Africa with the hope, which had been in-

creased by his success, that he should carry
home victory and not terms of peace. Still,
though he had victory in a manner within his
grasp, he would not refuse accommodation, that all
the nations might know that the Roman people
both undertake and conclude wars with justice."

The terms which he laid down were : the
restoration of all prisoners and deserters, the withdrawal of the Carthaginian armies from Italy and
Gaul and all the Mediterranean islands, the giving
up of all claim to Spain, the surrender of all their
warships except twenty. A considerable, but
not heavy, indemnity in grain and money was
also demanded. He gave them three days'
grace to decide whether to accept these terms,
adding that if they accepted they were to make
a truce with him and send envoys to the Senate
at Rome.

The moderation of these terms is remarkable,
especially considering the completeness of Scipio's
military success. It is a testimony not only to
Scipio's greatness of soul, but to his transcendent
political vision. Viewed in conjunction with
his similar moderation after Zama, it is not too
much to say that Scipio had a clear grasp of what
is just dawning on the mind of the world to-day—
that the true national object in war, as in peace,
is a more perfect peace. War is the result of a
menace to this policy, and is undertaken in order

to remove the menace, and by the subjugation of the will of the hostile State " to change this adverse will into a compliance with our own policy, and the sooner and more cheaply in lives and in money we can do this, the better chance is there of a continuance of national prosperity in the widest sense. The aim of a nation in war is, therefore, to subdue the enemy's will to resist with the least possible human and economic loss to itself." [1]   The lesson of history, of very recent history moreover, enables us to deduce this axiom, that " A military victory is not in itself equivalent to success in war." [2]   Further, as regards the peace terms, " the contract must be reasonable ; for to compel a beaten foe to agree to terms which cannot be fulfilled is to sow the seeds of a war which one day will be declared in order to cancel the contract." [2] There is only one alternative — annihilation. Mommsen's comment on Scipio's moderation over these terms is that they " seemed so singularly favourable to Carthage, that the question obtrudes itself whether they were offered by Scipio more in his own interest or in that of Rome."   A self-centred seeker after popularity

[1] 'Paris, or the Future of War,' by Captain B. H. Liddell Hart. 1925.
[2] 'The Foundations of the Science of War,' by Colonel J. F. C. Fuller. 1926.

would surely have prolonged the war to end it with a spectacular military decision, rather than accept the paler glory of a peace by agreement. But Mommsen's insinuation, as also his judgment, is contradicted by Scipio's similar moderation after Zama, despite the extreme provocation of a broken treaty.

These terms the Carthaginians accepted, and complied with the first provision by sending envoys to Scipio to conclude a truce and also to Rome to ask for peace, the latter taking with them a few prisoners and deserters, as a diplomatic promissory note. But the war party had again prevailed, and though ready to accept the peace negotiations as a cloak and a means of gaining time, they sent an urgent summons to Hannibal and Mago to return to Africa. The latter was not destined to see his homeland, for wounded just previously in an indecisive battle, he died of his injuries as his fleet of transports was passing Sardinia.

Hannibal, anticipating such a recall, had already prepared ships and withdrawn the main strength of his army to the port, keeping only his worst troops as garrisons for the Bruttian towns. It is said that no exile leaving his own land ever showed deeper sorrow than Hannibal on quitting the land of his enemies, and that he cursed himself that he had not led his troops on Rome when fresh from the victory of Cannæ. "Scipio," he said, "who had not looked at a Carthaginian enemy in Italy, had dared to go and attack Carthage, while he, after slaying a hundred thousand men at Trasimene and Cannæ, had suffered his strength to wear away around Casilinum, Cannæ, and Nola."

The news of his departure was received in Rome with mingled joy and apprehension, for the commanders in southern Italy had been ordered by the Senate to keep Hannibal in play, and so fix him while Scipio was securing the decision in Africa. Now, they felt that his presence in Carthage might rekindle the dying embers of the war and endanger Scipio, on whose single army the whole weight of the war would fall.

On the arrival of Lælius in Rome, amid uproarious scenes of jubilation, the Senate had decided that he should remain there until the Carthaginians' envoys arrived. With the envoys of Masinissa mutual congratulations were exchanged, and the Senate not only confirmed him in the title of King conferred by Scipio, but presented him by proxy with further presents of honour and the military trappings usually provided for a consul. They also acceded to his request to release their Numidian captives, a politic step by which he hoped to strengthen his hold on his countrymen.

When the envoys from Carthage arrived, they addressed the Senate in terms similar to those they had used to Scipio, putting the whole blame on Hannibal, and arguing that so far as Carthage was concerned the peace which closed the First Punic War remained unbroken. This being so they craved to continue the same peace terms. A debate followed in the Senate, which revealed a wide conflict of opinion, some advocating that no decision should be taken without the advice of Scipio, others that the war should at once be renewed, as Hannibal's departure suggested that the request for peace was a subterfuge. Lælius, called on for his opinion, said that Scipio had grounded his hopes of effecting a peace on the assurance that Hannibal and Mago would not be recalled from Italy. The Senate failed to come to a definite decision, and the debate was adjourned, though it would appear from Polybius that it was renewed later, and a settlement reached.

Meanwhile, however, the war had already restarted in Africa by a violation of the truce. While the embassy was on its way to Rome, fresh reinforcements and stores had been sent from Sardinia and Sicily to Scipio. The former arrived safely, but the convoy of two hundred transports from Sicily encountered a freshening gale when almost within sight of Africa, and though the warships struggled into harbour, the transports were blown towards Carthage ; the greater part to the island of Ægimurus—thirty miles distant at the mouth of the Bay of Carthage,—and the rest were driven on to the shore near the city. The sight caused great popular excitement, the people clamouring that such immense booty should not be missed. At a hasty assembly, into which the mob penetrated, it was agreed that Hasdrubal should cross over to Ægimurus with a fleet and seize the transports. After they had been brought in, those that had been driven ashore near Carthage were refloated and brought into harbour.

Directly Scipio heard of this breach of the truce he despatched three envoys to Carthage to take up the question of this incident, and also to inform the Carthaginians that the Roman people had ratified the treaty ; for despatches had just arrived for Scipio with this news. The envoys, after a strong speech of protest, delivered the message that while " the Romans would be justified in inflicting punishment, they entreated them in the name of the common fortune of mankind not to push the matter to an issue, but rather let their folly afford a proof of the generosity of the Romans." The envoys then retired for the Senate to debate. Resentment at the bold language of the envoys, reluctance to give up the ships and their supplies, new confidence from Hannibal's imminent help, combined to turn the scales against the peace party. It was decided simply to dismiss the envoys without a reply. The latter, who had barely escaped from mob violence on arrival, requested an escort on their return journey, and two triremes were assigned them. This fact gave some of the leaders of the war party an idea whereby to detonate a fresh explosion which should make the breach irreparable. They sent to Hasdrubal, whose fleet was then anchored off the coast near Utica, to have some ships lying in wait near the Roman camp to attack and sink the envoys' ship. Under orders, the commanders of the escort quitted the Roman quinquereme when within sight of the Roman camp. Before it could make the harbour it was attacked by three Carthaginian quadriremes despatched for the purpose. The attempt to board her was beaten off, but the crew, or rather the survivors, only saved themselves by running the ship ashore.

This dastardly action drove Scipio to renew operations for the final trial of strength. An immediate move direct on Carthage was impossible, for this would have meant a long siege, and to settle down to siege operations in face of the imminent arrival of Hannibal, who might menace his rear and cut his communications, would have been madness. Nor was his own situation pleasant, for not only had he suffered the heavy loss of the supplies and reinforcements from Sicily, but Masinissa was absent with his own and part of the Roman force—ten cohorts. Immediately on the conclusion of the provisional treaty Masinissa had set out for Numidia to recover his own kingdom, and, with the assistance of the Romans, add that of Syphax to it.

When the truce was broken, Scipio sent urgent and repeated messages to Masinissa, telling him to raise as strong a force as possible and rejoin him with all speed. Then, having taken measures for the security of his fleet, he deputed the command of the Roman base to his legate Bæbius, and started on a march up the valley of the Bagradas, aiming to isolate Carthage, and by cutting off all supplies and reinforcements from the interior undermine its strength as a preliminary to its direct subjugation—the principle of security once more. On his march, he no longer consented to receive the submission of towns which offered to surrender, but took them all by assault, and sold the inhabitants as slaves—to show his anger and impress the moral of the Carthaginians' violation of the treaty.

During this " approach " march—for such it was in fact if not in semblance—the envoys

returning from Rome reached the naval camp.
Bæbius at once despatched the Roman envoys
to Scipio, but detained the Carthaginians, who,
hearing of what had befallen, were naturally
distressed as to their own fate. But Scipio,
to his credit, refused to avenge on them the mal-
treatment of his own envoys. " For, aware as
he was of the value attached by his own nation
to keeping faith with ambassadors, he took
into consideration not so much the deserts of
the Carthaginians as the duty of the Romans.
Therefore restraining his own anger and the
bitter resentment he felt, he did his best to
preserve ' the glorious record of our fathers,'
as the saying is." He sent orders to Bæbius to
treat the Carthaginian envoys with all courtesy
and send them home. " The consequence was
that he humiliated all the people of Carthage
and Hannibal himself, by thus requiting in ampler
measure their baseness by his generosity."
(Polybius.)

In this act Scipio revealed his understanding
of the ethical object in war, and of its value.
Chivalry governed by reason is an asset both
in war and in view of its sequel—peace. Sensible
chivalry should not be confounded with the
quixotism of declining to use a strategical or
tactical advantage, of discarding the supreme
moral weapon of surprise, of treating war as

if it were a match on the tennis court—such quixotism as is typified by the burlesque of Fontenoy, " Gentlemen of France, fire first." This is merely stupid. So also is the traditional tendency to regard the use of a new weapon as " hitting below the belt," regardless of whether it is inhuman or not in comparison with existing weapons. So the Germans called the use of tanks an atrocity, and so did we term gas—so also the mediæval knight spoke of firearms when they came to interfere with his safe slaughter of unarmoured peasants. Yet the proportion of combatants slain in any battle decreased as much when firearms superseded the battleaxe and sword as when gas came to replace shell and the bullet. This antagonism to new weapons is mere conservatism, not chivalry.

But chivalry, as in this example of Scipio's, is both rational and far-sighted, for it endows the side which shows it with a sense of superiority, and the side which falls short with a sense of inferiority. The advantage in the moral sphere reacts on the physical.

If this chivalrous act of Scipio's was partly the fruit of such psychological calculation, it was clearly in accord also with his natural character, for his attitude earlier in Spain shows that it was no single theatrical gesture. Just as in war we cannot separate the moral from

L

the mental or physical spheres, so also in assessing character. We cannot separate the nobility of Scipio's moral conduct, throughout his career, from the transcendent clearness of his mental vision—they blended to form not only a great general but a great man.

Some time before this, probably during the episode which broke the truce, Hannibal had landed at Leptis—in what to-day is the Gulf of Hammamet—with twenty-four thousand men, and had moved to Hadrumetum. Stopping here [1] to refresh his troops, he sent an urgent appeal to the Numidian chief Tychæus, who " was thought to have the best cavalry in Africa," to join him in saving the situation. He sought to play on the fears of Tychæus, who was a relative of Syphax, by the argument that if the Romans won he would risk losing his dominion, and his life too, through Masinissa's greed of power. As a result, Tychæus responded, and came with a body of two thousand horse. This was a welcome accession, for Hannibal had lost his old superiority in cavalry, his master-weapon. In addition Hannibal could expect, and shortly received, the twelve thousand troops

---

[1] Livy says for a few days only, and Polybius is obscure on the point, but the known factors suggest a longer stay, because of the inevitable time required for the arrival of Tychæus's cavalry, and the junction with him of the other Carthaginian forces.

of Mago's force from Liguria, composed of Gauls
who had shown their fine quality in the last
battle before the recall; also a large body of
new levies raised in Africa, whose quality would
be less assuring.   Further—according to Livy,—
four thousand Macedonians had recently come
to the aid of Carthage, sent by King Philip.

Let this force once reach Carthage and be
able to base its operations on such a fortress,
and source of reinforcement, and the situation
would turn strongly in favour of Hannibal.
In contrast, Scipio had been robbed of the bulk
of his supplies and reinforcements, he was
isolated on hostile soil, part of his force was
detached with Masinissa, and the strength the
latter could recruit was still uncertain.

It is well to weigh these conditions, for they
correct common but false historical impressions.
At this moment the odds were with Hannibal,
and the feeling in the rival capitals, as recorded
by Livy and Polybius, is a true reflection of
the fact.

CHAPTER XI.

ZAMA.

EVEN at this critical juncture, jealousy of Scipio was rife in the Roman Senate. His backing, as all through, came from the people, not from his military rivals in the Senate. The consuls had done nothing to assist Scipio's campaign through fixing Hannibal in Italy, save that Servilius advanced to the shore after Hannibal was safely away. But at the beginning of the year when the allocation of the various provinces was decided, according to custom, both consuls pressed for the province of Africa, eager to reap the fruits of Scipio's success and thus earn glory cheaply. Metellus again tried to play the part of protecting deity. As a result the consuls were ordered to make application to the tribunes for the question to be put to the people to decide whom they wished to conduct the war in Africa. All the tribes thereupon nominated Scipio. Despite this emphatic popular verdict, the consuls drew lots for the province of Africa, having persuaded the Senate to make a decree to this effect. The lot fell to Tiberius Claudius, who was given an equal command with Scipio, and an armada of fifty quinqueremes for his expedition. Happily for Scipio, this jealousy-inspired move failed to prevent him putting the coping-stone on his own work, for Claudius was slow over his preparations, and when he eventually set out was caught in a storm and driven to Sardinia. Thus he never reached Africa.

Soon, too, as news of the changed situation in Africa filtered through, Scipio's detractors combined with the habitual pessimists in the distillation of gloom. They recalled that " Quintus Fabius, recently deceased, who had foretold how arduous the contest would be, had been accustomed to predict that Hannibal would prove a more formidable enemy in his own country than he had been in a foreign one ; and that Scipio would have to encounter not Syphax, a king of undisciplined barbarians . . . ; nor his father-in-law Hasdrubal, that most fugacious general " —a Fabian libel on a man of undaunted spirit ; " nor tumultuary armies hastily collected out of a crowd of half-armed rustics, but Hannibal . . . who, having grown old in victory, had filled Spain, Gaul, and Italy with monuments of his vast achievements ; who commanded troops of equal length of service ; troops hardened by superhuman endurance ; stained a thousand times with Roman blood. . . ." The tension in Rome was increased by the past years of indecisive warfare, carried on languidly and apparently endless, whereas now Scipio and Hannibal had stimulated the minds of all as generals prepared for a final death-clinch.

In Carthage the scales of public opinion appear to have been evenly balanced, on the one hand gaining confidence from Hannibal's achievements and invincibility, on the other depressed by reflection on Scipio's repeated victories, and on the fact that through his sole efforts they had lost their hold on Spain and Italy—as if he had been " a general marked out by destiny, and born, for their destruction."

On the threshold of this final phase, the support, moral and material, given to Hannibal by his country seems to have been, on balance, more than that accorded to Scipio—one more nail in the coffin of a common historical error.

His situation, already discussed, was one to test the moral fibre of a commander. Security lies often in calculated audacity, and an analysis of the military problems makes it highly probable that his march inland up the Bagradas valley was aimed, by its menace to the rich interior on which Carthage depended for supplies, to force Hannibal to push west to meet him instead of

north to Carthage. By this clever move he
threatened the economic base of Carthage and
protected his own, also luring Hannibal away
from his military base—Carthage.

A complementary purpose was that this line
of movement brought him progressively nearer
to Numidia, shortening the distance which Masinissa would have to traverse with his expected
reinforcement of strength. The more one studies
and reflects on this manœuvre, the more masterly
does it appear as a subtly blended fulfilment
of the principles of war.

It had the intended effect, for the Carthaginians sent urgent appeals to Hannibal to
advance towards Scipio and bring him to battle,
and although Hannibal replied that he would
judge his own time, within a few days he marched
west from Hadrumetum, and arrived by forced
marches at Zama. He then sent out scouts to
discover the Roman camp and its dispositions
for defence—it lay some miles farther west.
Three of the scouts, or spies, were captured,
and when they were brought before Scipio he
adopted a highly novel method of treatment.
" Scipio was so far from punishing them, as is
the usual practice, that on the contrary he
ordered a tribune to attend them and point out
clearly to them the exact arrangement of the
camp. After this had been done he asked them

if the officer had explained everything to their satisfaction. When they answered that he had done so, Scipio furnished them with provisions and an escort, and told them to report carefully to Hannibal what had happened to them" (Polybius). This superb insolence of Scipio's was a shrewd blow at the moral objective, calculated to impress on Hannibal and his troops the utter confidence of the Romans, and correspondingly give rise to doubts among themselves. This effect must have been still further increased by the arrival next day of Masinissa with six thousand foot and four thousand horse. Livy makes their arrival coincide with the visit of the Carthaginian spies, and remarks that Hannibal received this information, like the rest, with no feelings of joy.

The sequel to this incident of the scouts has a human interest of an unusual kind. " On their return, Hannibal was so much struck with admiration of Scipio's magnanimity and daring, that he conceived . . . a strong desire to meet him and converse with him. Having decided on this he sent a herald saying that he desired to discuss the whole situation with him, and Scipio, on receiving the herald's message, accepted and said that he would send to Hannibal, fixing a place and hour for the interview. He then broke up his camp and moved to a fresh site

not far from the town of Narragara, his position
being well chosen tactically, and having water
" within a javelin's throw." He then sent to
Hannibal a message that he was now ready for
the meeting. Hannibal also moved his camp
forward to meet him, occupying a hill safe and
convenient in every respect except that he was
rather too far away from water, and his men
suffered considerable hardship as a result. It
looks as if Scipio had scored the first trick in
the battle of wits between the rival captains!
The second trick also, because he ensured a battle
in the open plain, where his advantage in cavalry
could gain its full value. He was ready to trump
Hannibal's master-card.

On the following day both generals came out
of their camps with a small armed escort, and then,
leaving these behind at an equal distance, met
each other alone, except that each was attended
by one interpreter. Livy prefaces the account
of the interview with the remark that here met
" the greatest generals not only of their own
times, but of any to be found in the records
of preceding ages . . ."—a verdict with which
many students of military history will be inclined to agree, and even to extend the scope
of the judgment another two thousand years.

Hannibal first saluted Scipio and opened the
conversation. The accounts of his speech, as

of Scipio's, must be regarded as only giving its
general sense, and for this reason as also the
slight divergences between the different authorities may best be paraphrased, except for some
of the more striking phrases. Hannibal's main
point was the uncertainty of fortune—which,
after so often having victory almost within his
reach, now found him coming voluntarily to
sue for peace. How strange, too, the coincidence
that it should have been Scipio's father whom
he met in his first battle, and now he came to
solicit peace from the son! "Would that neither
the Romans had ever coveted possessions outside
Italy, nor the Carthaginians outside Africa,
for both had suffered grievously." However, the
past could not be mended, the future remained.
Rome had seen the arms of an enemy at her
very gates ; now the turn of Carthage had come.
Could they not come to terms, rather than
fight it out to the bitter end ? " I myself am
ready to do so, as I have learnt by actual experience how fickle Fortune is, and how by a
slight turn of the scale either way she brings
about changes of the greatest moment, as if
she were sporting with little children. But I
fear that you, Publius, both because you are
very young, and because success has constantly
attended you both in Spain and in Africa, and you
have never up to now at least fallen into the

counter-current of Fortune, will not be convinced by my words, however worthy of credit
they may be." Let Scipio take warning by
Hannibal's own example. "What I was at
Trasimene and at Cannæ, that you are this day."
"And now here am I in Africa on the point of
negotiating with you, a Roman, for the safety
of myself and my country. Consider this, I
beg you, and be not over-proud." " . . . What
man of sense, I ask, would rush into such danger
as confronts you now?" The chance of a single
hour might blot out all that Scipio had achieved
—let him remember the fate of Regulus, from
whom likewise the Carthaginians had sought
peace on African soil. Hannibal then outlined
his peace proposals—that Sicily, Sardinia, and
Spain should be definitely given up to Rome,
and Carthage confine her ambitions to Africa.
In conclusion he said that if Scipio felt a natural
doubt as to the sincerity of the proposals, after
his recent experience, he should remember that
these came from Hannibal himself, the real
power, who would guarantee so to exert himself
that no one should regret the peace. Hannibal
later was to prove both his sincerity and the
truth of this guarantee. But in the circumstances of the moment and of the past, Scipio
had good ground for doubt.

To Hannibal's overture he pointed out that it

was easy to express regret that the two powers had gone to war—but who had begun it ? Had Hannibal even proposed them before the Romans crossed to Africa, and voluntarily retired from Italy, his proposals would almost certainly have been accepted. Yet in spite of the utterly changed position, with the Romans " in command of the open country," Hannibal now proposed easier terms than Carthage had already accepted in the broken treaty. All he offered, in fact, was to give up territory which was already in Roman possession, and had been for a long time. It was futile for him to submit such empty concessions to Rome. If Hannibal would agree to the conditions of the original treaty, and add compensation for the seizure of the transports during the truce, and for the violence offered to the envoys, then he would have something to lay before his council. Otherwise, " the question must be decided by arms." This brief speech is a gem of clear and logical reasoning. Hannibal apparently made no advance on his former proposals, and the conference therefore came to an end, the rival commanders returning to their camps.

Both sides recognised the issues that hung upon the morrow—" the Carthaginians fighting for their own safety and the dominion of Africa, and the Romans for the empire of the world.

Is there any one who can remain unmoved in reading the narrative of such an encounter ? For it would be impossible to find more valiant soldiers, or generals who had been more successful and were more thoroughly experienced in the art of war, nor indeed had Fortune ever offered to contending armies a more splendid prize of victory " (Polybius). If the prize was great, so was the price of defeat. For the Romans if beaten were isolated in the interior of a foreign land, while the collapse of Carthage must follow if the army that formed her last bulwark was beaten. These crucial factors were stressed by the opposing commanders when next morning at daybreak they led out their troops for the supreme trial, and had made their dispositions.

Scipio rode along the lines and addressed his men in a few appropriate words. Polybius's account, though necessarily but the substance and not an exact record, is so in tune with Scipio's character as to be worth giving. " Bear in mind your past battles and fight like brave men worthy of yourselves and of your country. Keep it before your eyes that if you overcome your enemies not only will you be unquestioned masters of Africa, but you will gain for yourselves and your country the undisputed command and sovereignty of the rest of the world. But if the result of the battle be otherwise, those who have fallen bravely in the fight will be for ever shrouded in the glory of dying thus for their country, while those who save themselves by flight will spend the remainder of their lives in misery and disgrace. For no place in Africa will afford you safety, and if you fall into the hands of the Carthaginians it is plain enough to those who reflect what fate awaits you. May none of you, I pray, live to experience that fate, now that Fortune offers us the most glorious of prizes; how utterly craven, nay, how foolish shall we be, if we reject the greatest of goods and choose the greatest of evils from mere love of life. Go, therefore, to meet the foe with two objects before you, either victory or death. For men animated by such a spirit must always overcome their adversaries, since they go into battle ready to throw their lives away." Of this address Livy says "he delivered these remarks with a body so erect, and with a countenance so full of exultation, that one would have supposed that he had already conquered."

On the other side Hannibal ordered each commander of the foreign mercenaries to address his own men, appealing to their greed for booty, and bidding them be sure of victory from his presence and that of the forces he had brought back. With the Carthaginian levies he ordered their commanders to dwell on the sufferings of their wives and children should the Romans conquer. Then to his own men he spoke personally, reminding them of their seventeen years' comradeship and invincibility, of the victory of Trebia won over the father of the present Roman general, of Trasimene and Cannæ—" battles with which the action in which we are about to engage is not worthy of comparison." Speaking thus, he bade them cast their eyes on the opposing army and see for themselves that the Romans were fewer in numbers, and further, only a fraction of the forces they had conquered in Italy.

The dispositions made by the rival leaders have several features of note. Scipio placed his heavy Roman foot—he had probably two legions—in the centre ; Lælius with the Italian cavalry on the left wing, and on the right wing Masinissa with the whole of the Numidians, horse and foot, the latter presumably prolonging the centre and the cavalry on their outer flank.

The heavy infantry were drawn up in the normal three lines, first the *hastati*, then the *principes*, and finally the *triarii*. But instead of adopting the usual chequer formation, with the maniples of the second line opposite to and covering the intervals between the maniples of the first line, he ranged the maniples forming the rear lines directly behind the respective

maniples of the first line. Thus he formed wide
lanes between each cohort—which was primarily
composed of one maniple of *hastati*, one of *principes*, and one of *triarii*.

His object was twofold : on the one hand, to
provide an antidote to the menace of Hannibal's
war elephants and to guard against the danger
that their onset might throw his ranks into
disorder; on the other, to oil the working of his
own machine by facilitating the sallies and
retirements of his skirmishers. These *velites*
he placed in the intervals in the first line, ordering
them to open the action, and if they were forced
back by the charge of the elephants, to retire.
Even this withdrawal he governed by special
instructions, ordering those who had time to
fall back by the straight passages and pass
right to the rear of the army, and those who were
overtaken to turn right or left as soon as they
passed the first line, and make their way along
the lateral lanes between the lines. This wise
provision economised life, ensured smooth func-
tioning, and increased the offensive power—a
true fulfilment of economy of force. It may
even be termed the origin of modern extended
order, for its object was the same—to nega-
tive the effect of the enemy's projectiles by
creating empty intervals, a reduction of the
target by dispersion, the only difference being

THIRD PHASE
SCIPIO'S MANOEUVRE

SCIPIO
TRIARII PRINCIPES HASTATI

TRIARII PRINCIPES HASTATI

HANNIBAL

BATTLE OF ZAMA

CARTHAGINIAN   ELEPHANTS
INFANTRY
CAVALRY

ROMAN   LIGHT TROOPS (Velites)
INFANTRY MANIPLES
CAVALRY

TO ZAMA

HANNIBAL'S CAMP

TO SICCA

CARTHAGINIAN HORSE

LAELIUS

HANNIBAL

SCIPIO

NUMIDIAN HORSE

SCIPIO'S CAMP

MASINISSA

TO NARRAGARA

BRITISH MILES

0   ½   1

that Hannibal's projectiles were animal, not mineral.

The Carthaginian had eighty elephants, more than in any previous battle, and in order to terrify the enemy he placed them in front of his line. Supporting them, in the first line, were the Ligurian and Gallic mercenaries intermixed with Balearic and Moorish light troops. These were the troops with whom Mago had sailed home, about twelve thousand in number, and it is a common historical mistake to regard the whole force as composed of light troops.

In the second line Hannibal placed the Carthaginian and African levies as well as the Macedonian force, their combined strength probably exceeding that of the first line. Finally Hannibal's own troops formed the third line, held back more than two hundred yards distant from the others, in order evidently to keep it as an intact reserve, and lessen the risk of it becoming entangled in the mêlée before the commander intended. On the wings Hannibal disposed his cavalry, the Numidian allies on the left and the Carthaginian horse on the right. His total force was probably in excess of fifty thousand, perhaps fifty-five thousand. The Roman strength is less certain, but if we assume that each of Scipio's two legions was duplicated by an equal body of Italian allies, and add Masinissa's ten thousand, the complete strength would be about thirty-six thousand if the legions were at full strength. It was probably less, because some wastage must have occurred during the earlier operations since quitting his base.

The First Phase.—The battle opened, after preliminary skirmishing between the Numidian horse, with Hannibal's orders to the drivers of the elephants to charge the Roman line. Scipio promptly trumped his opponent's ace, by a tremendous blare of trumpets and cornets along the whole line. The strident clamour so startled and terrified the elephants that many of them at once turned tail and rushed back on their own troops. This was especially the case on the left wing, where they threw the Numidians, Hannibal's best cavalry wing, into disorder just as they were advancing to the attack. Masinissa seized this golden opportunity to launch a counter-stroke, which inevitably overthrew the disorganised opponents. With Masinissa in hot pursuit, they were driven from the field, and so left the Carthaginian left wing exposed.

The remainder of the elephants wrought much havoc among Scipio's *velites*, caught by their charge in front of the Roman line. But the foresight that had provided the " lanes " and laid down the method of withdrawal was justified by its results. For the elephants took the line of least resistance, penetrating into the lanes rather than face the firm-knit ranks of the heavy infantry maniples. Once in these lanes the *velites* who had retired into the lateral passages, between the lines, bombarded them with darts from both sides. Their reception was far too warm for them to linger when the door of escape was held wide open. While some of the elephants rushed right through, harmlessly, and out to the open in rear of the Roman army, others were driven back out of the lanes and fled towards the Carthaginian right wing. Here the Roman cavalry received them with a shower of javelins, while the Carthaginian cavalry could not follow suit, so that the elephants naturally trended towards the least unpleasant side. " It was at this moment that Lælius, availing himself of the disturbance created by the elephants, charged the Carthaginian cavalry and forced them to headlong flight. He pressed the pursuit closely, as likewise did Masinissa." Both Hannibal's flanks were thus stripped bare. The decisive manœuvre of Cannæ was repeated, but reversed.

Scipio was certainly an artist in tactical " boomerangs," as at Ilipa so now at Zama his foresight and art turned the enemy's best weapon back upon themselves. How decisive might have been the charge of the elephants is shown by the havoc they wrought at the outset among the *velites*.

The Second Phase.—In the meantime the infantry of both armies had " slowly and in imposing array advanced on each other," except that Hannibal kept his own troops back in their original position. Raising the Roman war-cry on one side, polyglot shouts on the other—this vocal discord was a moral drawback,—the lines met. At first the Gauls and Ligurians had the balance of advantage, through their personal skill in skirmishing and more rapid movement. But the Roman line remained unbroken, and the weight of their compact formation pushed the enemy back despite losses. Another factor told, for while the leading Romans were encouraged by the shouts from the rear lines, coming on to back them up, Hannibal's second line—the Carthaginians—failed to support the Gauls, but hung back in order to keep their ranks firm. Forced steadily back, and feeling they had been left in the lurch by their own side, the Gauls turned about and fled. When they tried to seek shelter in the second line, they were repulsed by the Carthaginians, who, with apparently sound yet perhaps unwise military instinct, deemed it essential to avoid any disarray which might enable the Romans to penetrate their line. Exasperated and now demoralised, many of the Gauls tried to force an opening in the Carthaginian ranks, but the latter showed that their courage was not deficient and drove them off. In a short time the relics of the first line had dispersed completely, or disappeared round the flanks of the second line. The latter confirmed their fighting quality by thrusting back the Roman first line—the *hastati* —also. In this they were helped by a human obstacle, the ground encumbered with corpses and slippery with blood, which disordered the ranks of the attacking Romans. Even the *principes* had begun to waver when they saw the first line driven back so decisively, but their officers rallied them and led them forward in the nick of time to restore the situation. This reinforcement was decisive. Hemmed in, because the Roman formation produced a longer frontage and so overlapped the Carthaginian line, the latter was steadily cut to pieces. The survivors fled back on the relatively distant third line, but Hannibal continued his policy of refusing to allow the fugitives to mix with and disturb an ordered line. He ordered the foremost ranks of his " Old Guard " to lower their spears as a barrier against them, and they were forced to retreat towards the flanks and the open ground beyond.

The Third Phase.—The curtain now rose on

what was practically a fresh battle. The Romans "had penetrated to their real antagonists, men equal to them in the nature of their arms, in their experience of war, in the fame of their achievements. . . ." Livy's tribute is borne out by the fierceness and the for long uncertain issue of the subsequent conflict, which gives the lie to those who pretend that Hannibal's "Old Guard" was but a shadow of its former power in the days of Trasimene and Cannæ.

The Romans had the moral advantage of having routed two successive lines, as well as the cavalry and elephants, but they had now to face a compact and fresh body of twenty-four thousand veterans, under the direct inspiration of Hannibal. And no man in history has shown a more dynamic personality in infusing his own determination in his troops.

The Romans, too, had at last a numerical advantage, not large, however—Polybius says that the forces were "nearly equal in numbers," —and in reality still less than it appeared. For, while all Hannibal's third line were fresh, on Scipio's side only the *triarii* had not been engaged, and these represented but half the strength of the *hastati* or *principes*. Further, the *velites* had been so badly mauled that they had to be relegated to the reserve, and the cavalry were off the field, engaged in the pursuit.

Thus it is improbable that Scipio had at his disposal for this final blow more than eighteen or twenty thousand infantry, less the casualties these had already suffered.

His next step is characteristic of the man—of his cool calculation even in the heart of a battle crisis. Confronted by this gigantic human wall—such the Carthaginians would appear in phalanx, —he sounds the recall to his leading troops, and it is a testimony to their discipline that they respond like a well-trained pack of hounds. Then in face of an enemy hardly more than a bow-shot distant he not only reorganises his troops but reconstructs his dispositions! His problem was this—against the first two enemy lines the Roman formation, shallower than the Carthaginian phalanx and with intervals, had occupied a wider frontage and so enabled him to overlap theirs. Now, against a body double the strength, his frontage was no longer, and perhaps less than Hannibal's. His appreciation evidently took in this factor, and with it two others. First, that in order to concentrate his missile shock power for the final effort it would be wise to make his line as solid as possible, and this could be done because there was no longer need or advantage for retaining intervals between the maniples. Second, that as his cavalry would be returning any moment, there was no advantage in keeping the orthodox formation in depth and using the *principes* and *triarii* as a direct support and reinforcement to his front line. The blow should be as con‑ centrated as possible in time and as wide as possible in striking force, rather than a series of efforts. We see him, therefore, making his *hastati* close up to form a compact centre without intervals. Then similarly he closes each half of his *principes* and *triarii* outwards, and advances them to extend the flank on either wing. The order from right to left of his now continuous line would thus be half the *triarii*, half the *principes*, the *hastati*, the other half of the *principes*, the other half of the *triarii*. He now once more overlaps the hostile front. To British readers this novel formation of Scipio's, inspired by a flash of genius in the middle of a momentous conflict, should have a special interest. For here is born the " line " which the Peninsular War and Waterloo have made immortal, here Scipio anticipated Wellington by two thousand years in revealing the truth that the long shallow line is the formation which allows of the greatest volume of fire, which fulfils the law of economy of force by bringing into play the fire—whether bullets or javelins—of the greatest possible pro‑ portion of the force. The rôle of Scipio's infantry in the final phase was to fix Hannibal's force

ready for the decisive manœuvre to be delivered
by the cavalry. For this rôle violence and
wideness of onslaught was more important than
sustenance. Scipio made his redistribution de-
liberately and unhurriedly—the longer he could
delay the final tussle the more time he gained for
the return of his cavalry. It is not unlikely
that Masinissa and Lælius pressed the pursuit
rather too far, and so caused an unnecessary
strain on the Roman infantry and on Scipio's
plan. For Polybius tells us that when the rival
infantries met " the contest was for long doubtful,
the men falling where they stood out of determination, until Masinissa and Lælius arrived
providentially at the proper moment." Their
charge, in the enemy's rear, clinched the decision,
and though most of Hannibal's men fought
grimly to the end, they were cut down in their
ranks. Of those who took to flight few escaped,
nor did the earlier fugitives fare any better,
for Scipio's cavalry swept the whole plain, and
because of the wide expanse of level country,
found no obstacle to their searching pursuit.

Polybius and Livy agree in putting the loss
of the Carthaginians and their allies at twenty
thousand slain and almost as many captured.
On the other side, Polybius says that " more
than fifteen hundred Romans fell," and Livy,
that " of the victors as many as two thousand

fell." The discrepancy is explained by the word
" Romans," for Livy's total clearly includes the
allied troops. It is a common idea among
historians that these figures are an underestimate,
and that in ancient battles the tallies given
always minimise the losses of the victor. Ardant
du Picq, a profound and experienced thinker,
has shown the fallacy of these cloistered historians. Even in battle to-day the defeated side
suffers its heaviest loss after the issue is decided,
in what is practically the massacre of unresisting
or disorganised men. How much more must
this disproportion have occurred when bullets,
still less machine-guns, did not exist to take
their initial toll of the victors. So long as forma-
tions remained unbroken the loss of life was
relatively small, but when they were isolated or
dissolved the massacre began.

" Hannibal, slipping off during the confusion
with a few horsemen, came to Hadrumetum,
not quitting the field till he had tried every
expedient both in the battle and before the
engagement ; having, according to the admission
of Scipio, acquired the fame of having handled
his troops on that day with singular judgment "
(Livy). Polybius's tribute is equally ungrudging :
" For, firstly, he had by his conference with
Scipio attempted to end the dispute by himself
alone ; showing thus that while conscious of

his former successes he mistrusted Fortune, and was fully aware of the part that the unexpected plays in war. In the next place, when he offered battle, he so managed matters that it was impossible for any commander to make better dispositions for a contest against the Romans than Hannibal did on that occasion. The order of a Roman force in battle makes it very difficult to break through, for without any change it enables every man individually and in common with his fellows to present a front in any direction, the maniples which are nearest to the danger turning themselves by a single movement to face it. Their arms also give the men both protection and confidence, owing to the size of the shield and owing to the sword being strong enough to endure repeated blows. . . . But nevertheless to meet each of these assets Hannibal had shown supreme skill in adopting . . . all such measures as were in his power and could reasonably be expected to succeed. For he had hastily collected that large number of elephants, and had placed them in front on the day of the battle in order to throw the enemy into confusion and break his ranks. He had placed the mercenaries in advance with the Carthaginians behind them, in order that the Romans before the final engagement might be fatigued by their exertions, and that their swords might lose their

edge . . . and also in order to compel the
Carthaginians thus hemmed in front and rear to
stand fast and fight, in the words of Homer :
' That e'en the unwilling might be forced to
fight.'

"The most efficient and steadfast of his troops
he had held in rear at an unusual distance in
order that, anticipating and observing from afar
the course of the battle, they might with un-
diminished strength and spirit influence the
battle at the right moment. If he, who had never
yet suffered defeat, after taking every possible
step to ensure victory, yet failed to do so, we
must pardon him. For there are times when
Fortune counteracts the plans of valiant men,
and again at times, as the proverb says, ' A
brave man meets another braver still,' as we
may say happened in the case of Hannibal."

Using this proverb in the sense that Polybius
clearly meant it, here in a brief phrase is our
verdict on the battle—a master of war had met
a greater master. Hannibal had no Flaminius
or Varro to face. No longer was a complacent
target offered him by a Roman general, conservative and ignorant of the "sublime part of
war" like those who first met Hannibal in
Italy, unwilling recipients of his instructional
course. At Zama he faced a man whose vision
had told him that in a cavalry superiority lay

the master-card of battle; whose diplomatic genius had led him long since to convert, in spirit and in effect, Hannibal's source of cavalry to his own use; whose strategic skill had lured the enemy to a battle-ground where this newly gained power could have full scope and offset his own numerical weakness in the other arms.

Rarely has any commander so ably illustrated the meaning of that hackneyed phrase " gaining and retaining the initiative." From the day when Scipio had defied the opinion of Fabius, monument of orthodoxy, and moved on Carthage instead of on the "main armed forces of the enemy," [1] he had kept the enemy dancing to his tune. Master in the mental sphere, he had compassed their moral disintegration to pave the way for the final act—their overthrow in the physical sphere. That this followed is less remarkable than the manner of its execution. Scipio is almost unique in that as a tactician he was as consummate an artist as in his strategy. Of few of the great captains can it be said that their tactical rivalled their strategical skill, or the reverse. Napoleon is an illustration. But in battle as in the wider field Scipio achieved

---

[1] Two thousand years later this is still the unshakable dogma of orthodox military opinion, despite the hard lessons of 1914-18, when the armies battered out their brains against the enemy's strongest bulwark.

that balance and blend of the mental, moral, and physical sphere which distinguishes him in the roll of history. Thus it came about that on the battlefield of Zama Scipio not only proved capable of countering each of Hannibal's points, but turned the latter's own weapon back upon himself to his mortal injury. Scan the records of time and we cannot find another decisive battle where two great generals gave of their best. Arbela, Cannæ, Pharsalus, Breitenfeld, Blenheim, Leuthen, Austerlitz, Jena, Waterloo, Sedan—all were marred by fumbling or ignorance on one side or the other.

CHAPTER XII.

AFTER ZAMA.

THE completeness of the victory left no room for a strategic pursuit, but Scipio did not linger in developing the moral exploitation of his victory. " Concluding that he ought to bring before Carthage everything which could increase the consternation already existing there . . . he ordered Gneius Octavius to conduct the legions thither by land ; and setting out himself from Utica with the fresh fleet of Lentulus added to his former one, made for the harbour of Carthage " (Livy). The immediate move achieved its object, a bloodless capitulation, thus crowning his eight years' fulfilment of the law of economy of force by saving the costly necessity of a siege.

A short distance from the harbour of Carthage he was met by a ship decked with fillets and branches of olive. " There were ten deputies, the leading men in the State, sent at the instance of Hannibal to solicit peace, to whom, when they had come up to the stern of the general's ship, holding out the badges of suppliants and entreating the protection and compassion of Scipio, the only answer given was that they must come to Tunis, whither he would move his camp. After taking a view of Carthage, not with any particular object of acquainting himself of it, but to dispirit the enemy, he returned to Tunis, and also recalled Octavius there" (Livy). The army on its way had received word that Vermina, the son of Syphax, was on his way to the succour of Carthage with a large force. But Octavius, employing a part of the infantry and all the cavalry, intercepted their march and routed them with heavy loss, his cavalry blocking all the routes of escape.

As soon as the camp at Tunis was pitched, thirty envoys arrived from Carthage, and to play on their fears they were kept waiting a day without an answer. At the renewed audience next day Scipio began by stating briefly that the Romans had no call to treat them with leniency, in view not only of their admission that they had begun the war, but of their recent treachery in violating a written agreement they had sworn to observe.

" But for our own sake and in consideration of the fortune of war and of the common ties of humanity we have decided to be clement and magnanimous. This will be evident to you also, if you estimate the situation rightly. For you should not regard it as strange if we impose hard obligations on you or if we demand sacrifices of you, but rather it should surprise you if we grant you any favours, since Fortune owing to your own misconduct has deprived you of any right to pity or pardon, and placed you at the mercy of your enemies." Then he stated first the indulgences, and next the conditions of peace —from that day onward the Romans would abstain from devastation or plunder ; the Carthaginians were to retain their own laws and customs, and to receive no garrison ; Carthage was to be restored all the territory in Africa that had been hers before the war, to keep all her flocks, herds, slaves, and other property. The conditions were—that reparation was to be made to the Romans for the injuries inflicted during the truce ; the transports and cargoes then seized were to be given up ; all prisoners and deserters were to be handed over. The Carthaginians were to surrender all their warships except ten triremes, all their elephants, and not to tame any more—Scipio evidently held these in more respect than some modern military historians do. The Carthaginians were not to make war at all on any nation outside Africa, and on no nation in Africa without consulting

Rome. They were to restore to Masinissa, within boundaries that should subsequently be settled, all the territory and property that had belonged to him or his forbears. They were to furnish the Roman army with sufficient corn for three months, and pay the troops until the peace mission had returned from Rome. They were to pay an indemnity of ten thousand talents of silver, in equal annual instalments spread over fifty years. Finally, they were to give as surety a hundred hostages, to be chosen by Scipio from their young men between fourteen and thirty years. The restoration of the transports was to be an immediate condition of a truce, " otherwise they would have no truce, nor any hope of peace."

202 B.C.—1919 A.D.! What moderation compared with the conditions of Versailles. Here was true grand strategy—the object a better peace, a peace of security and prosperity. Here were sown no seeds of revenge. The necessary guarantees of security were obtained by the surrender of the Carthaginian fleet, by the hostages, and by placing a strong and loyal watch-dog in Masinissa next door to Carthage. But they were kept down to the minimum both of cost to the conqueror and hardship to the con-quered. This cheaply afforded security paved the way for the future prosperity of Rome, and

at the same time made possible, justly, the revival of Carthage's prosperity.

The vindication of Scipio's generous and foresighted moderation lies in the fifty years of peace, unspotted on the Carthaginian side, which followed Zama. And had the Roman politicians been as wise and dispassionate as Scipio this peace would of a certainty have endured, with Carthage a prosperous and placid satellite of Rome, and the immortal phrase, *Delenda est Carthago,* instead of being translated into dreadful fact, would have been no more than the transitory hobby-horse of a senile " die-hard," a jest for a generation and then forgotten. Moreover, had the execution of the treaty terms been left with Scipio, there would not have been that malignant distortion of its clauses whereby constant complaints, but no more, were wrung from a long-suffering State. Even as it was, despite these constant petty inflictions, Carthage became as prosperous and populous as in the height of its power, and only by deliberate and outrageous provocation—the order to the citizens to destroy their own city—could these patient traders be forced into the revolt that afforded the desired pretext for their obliteration.

Let it be added that the moderation of Scipio called forth the response of Hannibal, and the true peace initiated by the former was being

faithfully fulfilled by the latter, until the un-
relenting hatred of the Roman Senate drove him
into exile from the country whose peaceful prosperity he was rebuilding. Not for the last time
in history, the vision and humanity of two great
rival soldiers gave a shining example of true
policy to revengeful and narrow-minded politicians. Yet for this constructive wisdom Hannibal paid by exile and forced suicide, Scipio
by ending his days in voluntary exile from a
State that had long since " dropped the pilot."
His envious and narrow political rivals in the
Senate could not refuse to ratify his peace terms
in face of his influence over the people, and
were for the moment too conscious of relief in
this happy ending of a ruinous and prolonged
struggle. But as the memory of danger passed,
and also of how narrowly they had escaped, these
checks on their hatred waned, and they could
not forgive " the man who had disdained to
punish more thoroughly the crime of having
made Romans tremble."

When Scipio had announced the terms of peace
to the envoys from Carthage, they carried them
at once to their Senate. His moderation did
not evoke an instant echo in an assembly that
was coincidently " indisposed for peace and unfit
for war." One of the Senators was about to
oppose the acceptance of the terms, and had

begun his speech when Hannibal came forward
and pulled him down from the tribune. The
other members became irate at this breach of
senatorial usage, whereupon Hannibal rose again,
and, admitting that he had been hasty, asked
their pardon for this " unparliamentary " conduct, saying, that as they knew, he had left
at nine years of age, and returned after thirty-
six years' absence on more practical debating.
He asked them to dwell rather on his patriotism,
for it was due to this that he had offended against
senatorial usage. " It seems to me astounding
and quite incomprehensible, that any man who
is a citizen of Carthage, and is conscious of the
designs that we all individually and as a body
have entertained against Rome, does not bless
his stars that now he is at the mercy of the
Romans he has obtained such lenient terms. If
you had been asked but a few days ago what you
expected your country to suffer in the event of
a Roman victory, you would not have been able
even to voice your fears, so extreme were the
calamities then in prospect. So now I beg you
not to argue the question, but to agree unanimously to the terms, and to pray, all of you,
that the Roman people may ratify the treaty." [1]

[1] While this is a Roman version of Hannibal's speech, the
comments ascribed to him are justified by the peace terms, and
it is unlikely that the Romans would give him undue credit for
a pacific influence.

This dust-dispelling breeze of common-sense so cleared their minds that they voted to accept the terms, and the Senate at once sent envoys with instructions to agree to them.

They had some difficulty in complying with the preliminary conditions for the truce, as although they could find the transports they could not return their cargoes, because much of the property was still in the hands of the irreconcilables. The envoys were forced to ask Scipio to accept a monetary compensation, and as he put no obstacles in the way, a three months' truce was settled and granted.

The envoys sent to Rome were chosen from the first men in the State—for the Romans had made it a ground of complaint that the former embassy lacked age and authority,—and they were further recommended to the Roman Senate by the inclusion of Hasdrubal Hædus, a consistent peace advocate and longstanding opponent of the Barcine party. This good impression he, as spokesman, developed by a speech that subtly flattered their dispassionate justice, and while tactfully admitting guilt, toned down its blackness.

The majority of the Senate were clearly in favour of peace, but Lentulus, who had succeeded to Claudius's consulship and also his ambition for cheap glory, protested against the deci-

sion of the Senate, as he had been canvassing
to be allotted Africa as his province, and hoped
that if he could keep alive the dying embers of
the war he might attain his ambition. But this
was promptly snuffed out, for when the question
was put to the assembly of the people, they
unanimously voted that the Senate should make
peace, that Scipio should be empowered to grant
it, and that he alone should conduct the army
home. The Senate therefore agreed accordingly,
and on the return of the Carthaginian envoys
peace was concluded on the terms set forth by
Scipio. The terms were punctually fulfilled, and
Scipio ordered the warships, five hundred in
number, to be towed out to the open sea and
there set on fire—the funeral pyre of Carthaginian
supremacy.

Scipio's enemies used in later years to insinuate
that the moderation of his terms was due to his
fear that harsher conditions might, by prolonging the war, force him to share his glory with a
successor. As this vulgar motive has also been
hinted at by some historians, it is worth while
to stress two facts which utterly demolish the
slander. First, the helplessness and passivity
of Carthage from that time onward ; second,
the way the Roman people squashed all attempts
to supersede him during this last phase. After
Zama, when all Rome was wild with enthusiasm,

no usurper, however pushful, would have stood the least chance of success.

Before leaving Africa, he first saw Masinissa established in his kingdom, and presented him with the lands of Syphax, delaying his own triumph in order to ensure the reward of his loyal assistants. Then at last, his task accomplished, he withdrew his army of occupation, and embarked them for Sicily. On arriving there he sent the bulk of his troops on by sea while he proceeded overland through Italy, one long triumphal procession, for not only did the people of every town turn out to do him honour, but the country folk thronged the roads. On arriving in Rome he " entered the city in a ' triumph ' of unparalleled splendour, and afterwards distributed to each of his soldiers four hundred *asses* out of the spoils." At this time, too, was born his surname of Africanus, " the first general who was distinguished by a name derived from the country which he had conquered." Whether this was bestowed by his soldiers, by his friends, or as a popular nickname is uncertain.

The enthusiasm of the people was so great that he could have obtained a title far more definite than any nickname, however distinguished. We know from a speech of Tiberius Gracchus, years later in the darkest hour of Scipio's career, that the people clamoured to make him perpetual consul and dictator, and that he severely rebuked them for striving to exalt him to what would have been, in reality if not in name, regal power. The authenticity of the fact is the more assured because Gracchus was then charging him with disregarding the authority of the tribunes. From this speech we also learn that Scipio "hindered statues being erected to him in the comitium, in the rostrum, in the Senate house, in the Capitol, in the chapel of Jupiter's temple, and that he prevented a decree being passed that his image, in a triumphal habit, should be brought in procession out of the temple of Jupiter. . . . Such particulars as these, which even an enemy acknowledged while censuring him . . . would demonstrate an uncommon greatness of mind, in limiting his honours conformably with his position as a citizen " (Livy).

Is there any other man in all history who has put aside so great a prize when it was not only within his reach but pressed upon him ? The incident of Cincinnatus returning to his farm after accomplishing his mission as dictator is immortal, yet Scipio's not only paralleled but eclipsed it. Which was the greater test—for a simple tribesman to conform to the traditions of a primitive State, or for a highly cultured and ambitious man of the world to eschew the virtual kingship of a supreme civilised power ? Compare, again, Scipio's action with the picture of Cæsar reluctantly refusing, in face of the groans of the multitude, the royal diadem which was offered by pre-arrangement with his supporters. In assessing the world's great figures, other than the definitely religious, we have tended to base our estimate mainly on concrete achievement and mental calibre, overlooking the moral values —the same lack of balance between the three spheres which has been remarked in the conduct of policy in peace and war. Even this test of achievement has been based on quantity rather than quality. That Cæsar's work is known universally, and Scipio little more than a name to the ordinary educated man, is a curious reflection on our historical standards, for the one inaugurated the world dominion of Roman civilisation, the other paved the way for its decay.

Extraordinary as is the nobility of mind which led Scipio to this self-abnegation, it becomes yet more so in view of his age. It is conceivable that a man in the last lap of life might have gained a philosophical outlook on the prizes of ambition, and spurned them from experience of their meretricious glitter. But that a man who at the early age of thirty-five had scaled the Himalayan peaks of achievement and fame should do so is

THE
MEDITERRANEAN WORLD

TERRITORY UNDER ROMAN
CONTROL in 210 B.C. WHEN SCIPIO
WAS APPOINTED TO COMMAND.

TERRITORY UNDER ROMAN
CONTROL AT END OF SCIPIOS
CAREER.

OCEANUS ATLANTICUS

GERMANIA

GALLIA

HISPANIA

CARPATHUS MONS

THRACIA

MACEDONIA

PONTUS EUXINUS

CAUCASUS MONS

ASSYRIA

MARE CASPIUM

SYRIA

CYPRUS

ARABIA

ALEXANDRIA

AEGYPTUS

THEBAE

SINUS ARABICUS

NILUS FL.

CRETA

MARE INTERNUM

AFRICA

NUMIDIA

SICILIA

SYRACUSAE

SARDINIA

CORSICA

ROMA

MARE ADRIATICUM

ATLAS MS.

MARE

CARTHAGO NOVA

PITYUSAE

BALEARES Is.

SAGUNTUM

TARRACO

PYRENEI MS

GADES

BRITISH MILES

0   50 100 200 300 400 500 600

a miracle of human nature. Little wonder that his countrymen gradually turned from adulation to petty criticism; little wonder that historians have forgotten him, for such loftiness of mind is beyond the comprehension of ordinary men— and ordinary men hate what they cannot understand.

CHAPTER XIII.

SIESTA.

AFTER being for eight of the most critical years of Rome's life the central figure, Scipio, for the remainder of his life, comes only at intervals into the limelight of history. He had saved Rome physically, and now by retiring into private citizenship he sought to save her morally. If a man who had attained such unapproachable heights of fame could sink his own ambition and interests, and show that the State was greater than the individual, the example might influence later generations. Supreme self-sacrifice has been one of the greatest moral forces in the civilisation of the world. But the force of Scipio's example was unhappily to be submerged by the self-seeking of such men as Marius, Sulla, and Cæsar.

To trace the latter and longer part of his career is difficult—the curtain is raised only on a series of brief scenes. We hear of him concerned with the resettlement of his soldiers; to each of his

Spanish and African veterans is allotted land in the proportion of two acres for every year's active service. Then three years after Zama he was elected censor, an office which was not only one of the higher magistracies, but regarded as the crown of a political career. As the title implies, the censors, two in number, conducted the census, which was not merely a registration but an occasion for checking the condition of public and private life. It was then that the censors issued edicts concerning the moral rules they intended to enforce, then that they punished irregularities of conduct, and then that they chose fresh members of the Senate. The censors were immune from responsibility for their acts, and the only limitation was that re-election was forbidden, and that no act was valid without the assent of both censors. Scipio's period of office seems to have been marked by unusual harmony, and a clean sheet as regards punishments.

We have to wait until 192 B.C. before we hear of him again, and once more the incident is an illuminating example of his generosity and breadth of view. In the seven years since the peace after Zama, Hannibal had been turning his genius into new channels—the restoration of Carthage's prosperity and the improvement of its administration. But in this labour he incurred the hostility

of many of his own countrymen. In his efforts
to safeguard the liberty of the people he stopped
the abuse of the judicial power—an abuse which
recalls the worst days of Venice. Similarly,
finding that the revenue could not raise the
annual payment to Rome without fresh taxation,
he made an investigation into the embezzlement
which lay at the root of this faulty administration. Those who had been plundering the public
combined with the order of judges to instigate the
Romans against Hannibal. The Romans, whose
fear of the great Carthaginian had not faded, had
been watching with envy and distrust the commercial revival of Carthage. They eagerly seized
on such a pretext for intervention. From Livy,
however, we learn that " a strenuous opposition
was for long made to this by Scipio Africanus,
who thought it highly unbecoming the dignity
of the Roman people to make themselves a party
to the animosities and charges against Hannibal ;
to interpose the public authority in the faction
strife of the Carthaginians, not deeming it sufficient to have conquered that commander in the
field, but to become as it were his prosecutors
in a judicial process. . . ." Scipio's opposition
delayed but it could not stop the lust for revenge
of smaller men—Cato was consul,—and an embassy was sent to Carthage to arraign Hannibal.
He, realising the futility of standing his trial,

decided to escape before it was too late, and sailed for Tyre, lamenting the misfortunes of his country oftener than his own.

At the beginning of the next year Scipio was elected consul for the second time, and his election along with Tiberius Longus afforded a coincidence in that their fathers had been consuls together in the first year of the Hannibalic war. Scipio's second consulship was comparatively uneventful, at least in a military sense, for the Senate decided that as there was no immediate foreign danger both consuls should remain in Italy. To this decision Scipio was strongly opposed, though he bowed to it, and once again history was to confirm his foresight and rebuke the " wait and see " policy of the near-sighted Roman Senators.

During the interval between Zama and his second consulship, Rome had been engaged in a struggle in Greece. The freedom of action which Zama conferred had combined with certain earlier factors to re-orient, or more literally to orient, her foreign policy. Ever since the repulse of Pyrrhus, Rome had been driving towards an inevitable contact with the Near East. Here the three great powers were the empires into which after Alexander the Great's death his vast dominion had been divided—Macedon, Egypt, and Syria, or, as it was then termed, Asia.

With Egypt, Rome had made an alliance eighty years before, and this alliance had been cemented by commercial ties. But Philip V. of Macedon had allied himself with Hannibal, and though his help was verbal rather than practical, the threat of an attack on Italy had driven the Romans to take the offensive against him, with the aid of a coalition of the Greek States. The drain on her resources elsewhere made Rome seize the first chance, in 205 B.C., for an indecisive peace. Taking advantage of her preoccupation with Hannibal, Philip made a compact with Antiochus of Syria to seize on and share the dominions of Egypt.

But after Zama, Rome was free to respond to the appeal of her ally, and eager also to take revenge for Philip's unneutral act in sending four thousand Macedonians to aid Hannibal in the final battle. The Senate, however, could only persuade the assembly of the people—anxious to enjoy the fruits of peace—by pretending that Philip was on the point of invading Italy. At Cynoscephalæ the legion conquered the phalanx, and Philip was forced to accept terms which reduced him to a second-rate power—like Carthage, stripped of his foreign possessions, and forbidden to make war without the consent of Rome.

The Roman Senate did not realise, however,

that this removal of the Macedonian danger made war inevitable with Antiochus of Syria, for the tide of Roman dominion clearly threatened his own submersion sooner or later. Rome had in effect swallowed first Carthage and then Macedon, and Antiochus had no liking for the rôle of Jonah. The Mediterranean world was too small to hold them both. Antiochus, inflated with his own grandiloquent title of "King of Kings," decided to take the initiative and enlarge his own dominions while the opportunity was good. In 197-196 B.C. he overran the whole of Asia Minor, and even crossed into Thrace.

Greece was obviously his next objective, but the Romans could not see this, though Scipio did. In a prophetic speech he declared "that there was every reason to apprehend a dangerous war with Antiochus, for he had already, of his own accord, come into Europe; and how did they suppose he would act in future, when he should be encouraged to a war, on one hand by the Ætolians, avowed enemies of Rome, and stimulated, on the other, by Hannibal, a general famous for his victories over the Romans?"—for Hannibal had recently moved to the court of Antiochus. But the Senate, acting like the proverbial ostrich, rejected this advice, and decided that not only should no new army be sent to Macedonia, but that the one which was there

o

should be brought home and disbanded. Had Scipio been allotted Macedonia as his province, the danger from Antiochus might have been nipped in the bud and the subsequent invasion of Greece prevented.

Politically, the main feature of his year of office was a wide extension of the policy of settling colonies of Roman citizens throughout Italy—a safeguard against such a dangerous revolt of the Italian States as had followed the invasion of Hannibal. Scipio himself enjoyed the honour of being nominated by the censors as prince of the Senate, an office which apart from its honour had greater influence than that of president, which it had replaced. For the president's functions were limited to those of the modern " Speaker," whereas the prince of the Senate could express his opinions as well as presiding.

The only serious hostilities during this year were in north-western Italy, where the Insubrian and Ligurian Gauls and the Boii had made one of their periodical risings. Longus, the other consul, whose province it was, moved against the Boii. Finding how strong and determined were their forces, he sent post-haste to Scipio, asking him, if he thought proper, to join him. The Gauls, however, seeing the consul's defensive attitude and guessing the reason, attacked at once before Scipio could arrive. It is evident that the Romans narrowly escaped a disaster, but the battle was sufficiently indecisive for them to retire unmolested to Placentia on the Po, while the Gauls withdrew to their own country.

The sequel is obscure, though some writers say that Scipio, after he had joined forces with his colleague, overran the country of the Boii and Ligurians as far as the woods and marshes allowed him to proceed. In any case he went there, for it is stated that he returned from Gaul to hold the elections. One other incident of his term of office was that, on his proposal, the Senators were for the first time allotted reserved and separate seats at the Roman games. While many held that this was an honour which ought to have been accorded long before, others opposed it vehemently, contending that " every addition made to the grandeur of the Senate was a diminution of the dignity of the people," that it distilled class feeling, and if the ordinary seats had been good enough for five hundred and thirty-eight years, why should a change be made now. " It is said that even Africanus himself at last became sorry for having proposed that matter in his consulship : so difficult is it to bring people to approve of any alteration of long-standing customs " (Livy).

All very petty ; and yet Scipio's good-natured

consideration for the comfort and dignity of others—it could not enhance his own—may have contributed to weaken his old influence with the people, who had been his support against the short-sighted Senators.

After the election of his successors, Scipio retired once more into private life, instead of taking a foreign province, as retiring consuls so often did. This circumstance has led one or two of the latter Roman historians to search for a motive. Thus Cornelius Nepos, the biographer of Cato, says that Scipio wanted to remove Cato from his province of Spain and become his successor, and that failing to obtain the Senate's assent, Scipio, to show his displeasure, retired into private life when his consulship was ended. Plutarch also, in his life of Cato, contradicts this, and says that Scipio actually succeeded Cato in Spain. Apart from the known historical inaccuracies of both these later writers, such pettiness would be inconsistent with all the assured facts of Scipio's character. We know that Cato and Scipio were always at variance, but the animosity, so far as speeches are recorded, was all on the side of Cato, to whom Scipio's Greek culture was as a red rag to a bull, and not less his moderation towards Carthage. The man whose parrot cry was *Delenda est Carthago*—fit ancestry of the Yellow Press—could not brook the man whose loftier soul and reputation stood in his way, nor his narrow spirit rest until he had brought about the destruction both of Carthage and Scipio. Their quarrel, if one-sided spite can be so called, dated from Zama, when Cato—serving as quæstor under Scipio, and already hating his Greek habits so much that he would not live in the same quarters—took violent exception to his general's lavish generosity to the soldiers in the distribution of the spoil.

Fortunately there are external facts which demolish the statements of both Nepos and Plutarch on this matter. A decision to disband Cato's army in Spain was made by the Senate at the same time as they refused Scipio's request to allot Macedonia as his consular province, and disbanded that army also. Cato accordingly returned, and received a triumph at the outset of Scipio's consulship. As there was no army there was obviously no post for a proconsul, which shows the futility of the statement that Scipio desired to go to Spain at the end of his consulship.

His real motive, however, in staying at Rome instead of seeking some other foreign province is not difficult to guess. He had predicted the danger from Antiochus, and as the Senate's refusal to anticipate it made a struggle inevitable, Scipio would wish to be on hand, ready for the call that he felt sure would come. He was right, for Hannibal was even then proposing to Antiochus an expedition against Italy, maintaining as ever that a campaign in Italy was the only key to Rome's defeat, because such invasion crippled the full output of Rome's man-power and resources. As a preliminary Hannibal proposed that he should be given a force to land in Africa and raise the Carthaginians, while Antiochus moved into Greece and stood by, ready for a spring across to Italy when the moment was ripe.

An envoy of Hannibal's, a Tyrian called Aristo, was denounced by the anti-Hannibalic party at Carthage. Aristo escaped, but the discovery caused such internal dissension that Masinissa thought the moment ripe to encroach on their territory.

The Carthaginians sent to Rome to complain, and he also to justify himself. The embassy of the former aroused uneasiness by their account of Aristo's mission and escape, and the envoys of Masinissa fanned this flame of suspicion. The Senate decided to send a commission to investigate, and Scipio was nominated one of the three, but after making an inquiry "left everything in suspense, their opinions inclining neither to one side or the other." This failure to give a verdict is hardly to the credit of Scipio, who had the knowledge and the influence with both

parties to have settled the controversy on the
spot. But Livy hints that the commissioners
may have been acting on instructions from the
Senate to abstain from a settlement, and adds
that in view of the general situation " it was
highly expedient to leave the dispute unde-
cided." By this he presumably means that as
Hannibal was meditating an invasion it was
policy to keep the Carthaginians too occupied to
support him.

At the end of the year an incident occurred
that sheds a significant light—rather twilight—
on Scipio's career. The two candidates for the
patrician vacancy as consul were Lucius Quinctius
Flamininus, brother of the victor of Cynoscephalæ, and Publius Cornelius Scipio, namesake
and half-brother to Africanus.

The upshot is aptly told by Livy : " Above
everything else, the brothers of the candidates,
the two most illustrious generals of the age,
increased the violence of the struggle. Scipio's
fame was the more splendid, and in proportion
to its greater splendour, the more obnoxious to
envy. That of Quinctius was the most recent,
as he had received a ' triumph ' that same year.
Besides, the former had now for almost two years
been continually in people's sight ; which circumstance, by the mere effect of satiety, causes
great characters to be less revered."   " All

Quinctius's claims to the favour of the public were fresh and new; since his triumph, he had neither asked nor received anything from the people; ' he solicited votes,' he said, ' in favour of his own brother, not of a half-brother; in favour of his *legatus* and partner in the conduct of the war ' "—his brother having commanded the fleet against Philip of Macedon. " By these arguments he carried his point." Lucius Quinctius was elected, and Scipio Africanus received a further rebuff when Lælius, his old comrade and lieutenant, failed to secure election as plebeian consul despite Scipio's canvassing. The crowd, eternally fickle and forgetful, preferred the rising star to the setting sun.

Meantime the war clouds were gathering in the East. Antiochus had safeguarded his rear by marrying his daughter to Ptolemy, King of Egypt. He then advanced to Ephesus, but lost time by waging a local campaign with the Pisidians. Across the Ægean, the Ætolians were labouring hard to stir up war against the Romans, and to find allies for Antiochus. Rome, on the contrary, was weary and exhausted with years of struggle, and sought by every means to postpone or avert a conflict with Antiochus. To this end the Senate sent an embassy to him, and Livy states that, according to the history written in Greek by Acilius, Scipio Africanus was employed on this mission. The envoys went to Ephesus, and while halting there on their way " took pains to procure frequent interviews with Hannibal, in order to sound his intentions, and to remove his fears of danger threatening him from the Romans." These meetings had the accidental and indirect but important consequence that the report of them made Antiochus suspicious of Hannibal.

But the main interest to us of these interviews, assuming that Acilius's witness is reliable, is the account of one of the conversations between Scipio and Hannibal. In it Scipio asked Hannibal, " Whom he thought the greatest captain ? " The latter answered, " Alexander . . . because with a small force he defeated armies whose numbers were beyond reckoning, and because he had overrun the remotest regions, merely to visit which was a thing above human aspirations." Scipio then asked, " To whom he gave the second place ? " and Hannibal replied, " To Pyrrhus, for he first taught the method of encamping, and besides no one ever showed such exquisite judgment in choosing his ground and disposing his posts ; while he also possessed the art of conciliating mankind to himself to such a degree that the natives of Italy wished him, though a foreign prince, to hold the sovereignty among them, rather than the Roman people. . . ."

On Scipio proceeding to ask, " Whom he esteemed
the third ? " Hannibal replied, " Myself, beyond
doubt." On this Scipio laughed, and added,
" What would you have said if you had conquered me ? " " Then I would have placed
Hannibal not only before Alexander and Pyrrhus,
but before all other commanders."

" This answer, turned with Punic dexterity,
and conveying an unexpected kind of flattery,
was highly grateful to Scipio, as it set him apart
from the crowd of commanders, as one of incom-
parable eminence."

From Antiochus this embassy gained no direct
result, for the " king of kings " was too swollen
with pride on account of his Asiatic successes,
too sure of his own strength, to profit by the
examples of Carthage and Macedon. His standards of military measurement were strictly quan-
titative.

Realising at last that war was inevitable and
imminent, the Roman Senate set about the
preparations for this fresh struggle. As a first
step they pre-dated the consular election so as
to be ready for the coming year ; the new consuls
were Publius Scipio, the rejected of the previous
year, and Manius Acilius. Next, Bæbius was
ordered to cross over with his army from Brundisium (Brindisi) into Epirus, and envoys were
sent to all the allied cities to counteract Ætolian

propaganda. The Ætolians, nevertheless, gained some success by a mixture of diplomacy and force, and besides causing general commotion throughout Greece, did their best to hasten the arrival of Antiochus. Had his energy approximated to his confidence, he might well have gained command of Greece before the Romans were able to thwart him. Further, to his own undoing, he abandoned Hannibal's plan and the expedition to Africa, from a jealousy inspired fear that if Hannibal were given an executive rôle public opinion would regard him as the real commander. Even when he made his belated landing in Greece, with inadequate forces, he missed such opportunity as was left by frittering away his strength and time in petty attacks against the Thessalian towns, and in idle pleasure at Chalcis.

Meantime, at Rome the consuls cast lots for their provinces; Greece fell to Acilius, and the expeditionary force which he was to take assembled at Brundisium. For its supply, commissaries had been sent to Carthage and Numidia to purchase corn. It is a tribute alike to the spirit in which the Carthaginians were seeking to fulfil their treaty with Rome, and to Scipio's wise policy after Zama, that they not only offered the corn as a present, but offered to fit out a fleet at their own expense, and to pay in a lump sum the annual tribute money for many years ahead. The Romans, however, whether from proud self-reliance or dislike of being under an obligation to Carthage, refused the fleet and the money, and insisted on paying for the corn.

In face of all these preparations, Antiochus awoke to his danger too late. His allies, the Ætolians, provided only four thousand men, his own troops delayed in Asia, and in addition he had alienated Philip of Macedon, who stood firm on the Roman side. With a force only ten thousand strong he took up his position at the pass of Thermopylæ, but failed to repeat the heroic resistance of the immortal Spartans, and was routed. Thereupon, forsaking his Ætolian allies to their fate, Antiochus sailed back across the Ægean.

Rome, however, was unwilling to rest content with this decision. She realised that in Greece her army had defeated only the advanced guard and not the main body of Antiochus's armed strength, and that unless he was subdued he would be a perpetual menace. Further, so long as he dominated Asia Minor from Ephesus, her loyal allies, the Pergamenes and Rhodians, and the Greek cities on the Asiatic side of the Ægean, were at his mercy. All these motives impelled Rome to counter-invasion.

Once more Hannibal's grand strategical vision

proved right, for he declared that " he rather wondered the Romans were not already in Asia, than had doubts of their coming." This time Antiochus took heed of his great adviser, and strengthened his garrisons as well as maintaining a constant patrol of the coast.

CHAPTER XIV.

THE LAST LAP.

ROME, faced with a great emergency—second only to that of the Hannibalic War,—looked for its new saviour in its old. If the danger was less, and less close, the risk at least must have seemed greater, for her armies were venturing into the unknown. The first great trial of strength between Rome and Asiatic civilisation was about to be staged, and the theatre of war was alarmingly distant, connected with the homeland by long and insecure lines of communication. The spur of emergency quickens the memory, and Rome in her fresh hour of trial remembered the man who had saved her in the last, and who had been standing by for several years ready for the occasion which he had prophesied to deaf ears. Yet Scipio Africanus did not himself stand for the consulship—why it is difficult to guess. It may have been that he deemed the forces of jealousy too strong, and wanted to take no risks, or that affection and sympathy for his brother

Lucius, a defeated candidate the year before, inspired Africanus to give the latter his chance. Africanus had glory enough, and all through his career he had been ready to share his glory with his assistants. He left envy of others' fame to lesser men. His aim was service, and in any case he knew that if Lucius was consul, he himself would exercise the real power—Lucius was welcome to the nominal triumph.

His brother's election was secured, and with him, as plebeian consul, was elected Gaius Lælius, the old assistant of Africanus. It may be that Scipio worked for this, in order to ensure that to whichever Greece fell as a province he would be able to exercise an influence on the operations. As it happened, however, the double election put him in the unpleasant position of having to support his brother against his friend. For both consuls naturally desired Greece, which meant the command against Antiochus. Lælius, who had a powerful interest with the Senate, asked the Senate to decide—drawing lots was too uncertain for his taste. Lucius Scipio thereupon asked time to seek advice, and consulted Africanus, "who desired him to leave it unhesitatingly to the Senate." Then, when a prolonged debate was anticipated, Africanus arose in the Senate and said that "if they decreed that province to his brother, Lucius Scipio, he would go along with him as his lieutenant." This proposal "being received with almost universal approbation," settled the dispute and was carried by an almost unanimous vote.

Though it is clear that Africanus planned this result, the fact does not lessen our appreciation of the nobility of a man who, after being the most illustrious commander in Rome's history, would stoop to take a subordinate position. If the means was diplomatic, the motive was of the purest—to save his country, leaving to another the reward. Apart from blood ties, he doubtless felt more sure of real control through his brother than through Lælius—though Lucius's obstinacy with the Ætolians refutes Mommsen's verdict that he was "a man of straw." Two good leaders in the same command are not a good combination. It says much for both Scipio Africanus and Lælius that this act did not break down their friendship, and it is a proof of the latter's generous nature, if also of the former's transcendent qualities, that in later years Lælius gave Polybius such testimony of Scipio's greatness.

In addition to the two legions which he was to take over in Greece from Acilius, the consul was given three thousand Roman foot and one hundred horse, and another five thousand foot and two hundred horse from the Latin confederates. Further, directly it was known that Africanus was going, four thousand veterans of the Hannibalic War volunteered in order to serve again " under their beloved leader."

The expedition set forth in March (the Roman July), 190 B.C., but the advance into Asia was to be delayed because of the Senate's obstinacy in refusing to grant reasonable peace terms to the Ætolians, so driving them to take up arms anew and maintain a stubborn warfare in their mountain strongholds. It is curious that Scipio, who had always contributed to his military object by the moderation of his political demands, should now be blocked by others' immoderation.

When the Scipios landed in Epirus they found their destined army thoroughly embroiled by Acilius in this guerilla warfare. Africanus went ahead while his brother followed with his main body. On arrival at Amphissa, Athenian envoys met them, who, addressing first Africanus and afterwards the consul, pleaded for leniency to the Ætolians. " They received a milder answer from Africanus, who, wishing for an honourable pretext for finishing the Ætolian war, was directing his view towards Asia and King Antiochus." Apparently Africanus, with his habitual foresight, had actually inspired this mission of the Athenians, and another to the Ætolians. Scipio could have given points even to Colonel

P

House as an ambassador of peace as a means to victory. As a result of Athenian persuasion, the Ætolians sent a large embassy to the Roman camp, and from Africanus received a most encouraging reply. But when the decision was referred to the consul, as was necessary, his reply was uncompromising—he put his fist through the web his brother had so delicately woven. A second embassy met with the same obstinate refusal. Then the principal Athenian envoy advised the Ætolians to ask simply for a six months' armistice in order that they might send an embassy to Rome. The real source of this advice is too obvious to require any guess. Accordingly the Ætolian envoys came back, and "making their first application to Publius Scipio, obtained, through him, from the consul a suspension of arms for the time they desired."

Thus by diplomacy Africanus secured his lines of communication and released his army; the determination with which he sought a peaceful solution, and avoided being embroiled in a side-show, is an object-lesson in economy of force and the maintenance of the true objective.

The consul, having taken over the army from Acilius, decided to lead his troops into Africa through Macedonia and Thrace—taking the long land instead of the short sea route, because Antiochus had one fleet at Ephesus and another being raised by Hannibal in Phœnicia specially to prevent their crossing by sea. Africanus, while approving of this route, told his brother that everything depended on the attitude of Philip of Macedon ; "for if he be faithful to our Government he will afford us a passage, and all provisions and material necessary for an army on a long march. But if he should fail you in this, you will find no safety in any part of Thrace. In my opinion, therefore, the King's dispositions ought to be ascertained first of all. He will best be tested if whoever is sent comes suddenly upon him, instead of by pre-arrangement."

Acting on this advice, as instinct with security as with psychology, Tiberius Gracchus, a specially active young man, was sent, riding by relays of horses, and so fast that he travelled from Amphissa to Pella—from the Gulf of Corinth almost to Salonika—in under three days, and caught Philip in the middle of a banquet—"far gone in his cups." This helped to remove suspicion that he was planning any counter-move, and next day Gracchus saw provision dumps prepared, bridges made over rivers, and hill roads buttressed—ready for the coming of the Roman army.

He then rode back to meet the army, which was thus able to move through Macedonia with confidence. On their passage through his domains Philip met and accompanied them, and Livy relates that " much geniality and good humour appeared in him, which recommended him much to Africanus, a man who, as he was unparalleled in other respects, was not averse to courteousness unaccompanied by luxury." The army then pushed on through Thrace to the Hellespont— the Dardanelles,—taking the same route apparently as Xerxes, in an opposite direction.

Their crossing of the Dardanelles had been smoothed for them as much by the mistakes of Antiochus as by the action of their own fleet. Livius, the Roman naval commander, had sailed for the Dardanelles, in accordance with instructions, in order to seize the fortress which guarded the passage of the Narrows. Sestos— modern Maidos—was already occupied, and Abydos—now Chanak—parleying for surrender, when news reached Livius of the surprise and defeat of the allied Rhodian fleet at Samos. He abandoned his primary object—an action which might have upset Scipio's plans—and sailed south to restore the naval situation in the Ægean. However, after some rather aimless operations, the arrival of Hannibal's fleet and its defeat—in his first and last sea battle—cleared the situation in the Mediterranean. A second victory in August, this time over Antiochus's

Ægean fleet, ensured for the Romans command of the sea.

With Antiochus, the loss of it led him into a move, intended for safety, that was actually the reverse. Despairing of being able to defend his possessions across the Dardanelles, he ordered the garrison to retire from Lysimachia, "lest it should there be cut off by the Romans." Now Lysimachia stood close to where Bulair stands to-day, and there is no need to emphasise how difficult it would have been to force those ancient Bulair Lines, commanding the isthmus of the Gallipoli peninsula. The garrison might well have held out till winter. Perhaps another factor, apart from the naval defeat, was his failure to gain the alliance of Prusias, King of Bithynia—a country whose sea coast lay partly on the Black Sea and partly on the Sea of Marmora. Antiochus sent to play on his fears of being swallowed by Rome, but once again Scipio's grand strategical vision had led him to foresee this move and take steps to checkmate it. Months before he reached Gallipoli, Scipio had written a letter to Prusias to dispel any such fears. "The petty chieftains in Spain," he wrote, "who had become allies, he had left kings. Masinissa he had not only re-established in his father's kingdom, but had put him in possession of that of Syphax "—a clever hint !

The double news of the naval victory and the evacuation of Lysimachia reached the Scipios on arrival at Ænos (Enos), and, considerably relieved, they pressed forward and occupied the city. After a few days' halt, to allow the baggage and sick to overtake them, they marched down the Chersonese—the Gallipoli peninsula,—arrived at the Narrows, and made an unopposed crossing. They crossed, however, without Africanus, who was detained behind by his religious duties as one of the Salian priests. The rules of his order compelled him during this festival of the Sacred Shields to remain wherever he was until the month was out—and without Africanus the army had lost its dynamo, so that "he himself was a source of delay, until he overtook the rest of the army." Unnecessary delay was far from one of his military characteristics, so that the incident serves to suggest that his piety was genuine and not merely a psychological tool to inspire his troops. While the army was waiting for him, an envoy came to the camp from Antiochus, and as he had been ordered by the king to address Africanus first, he also waited for him before discussing his mission!

"In him he had the greatest hope, besides that his greatness of soul, and the fulness of his glory, tended very much to make him inclined to peace, and it was known to all nations what

sort of a conqueror he had been, both in Spain
and afterwards in Africa; and also because his
son was then a prisoner with Antiochus" (Livy).
How the son was captured is uncertain, whether
in a distant cavalry reconnaissance, or earlier
at sea, as Appian suggests.

At a full council the Syrian envoy put forward
a basis for peace—that Antiochus would give
up the Greek cities in Asia Minor allied to Rome,
as he had already evacuated Europe, and would
pay the Romans half the expenses of the war.
The council regarded these concessions as inadequate, contending that Antiochus should
give up all the Greek seaboard on the Ægean,
and, in order to establish a wide and secure
neutral zone, relinquish possession of all Asia
Minor west of the Taurus mountains. Further,
he ought to pay all the expense of the war, as
he had caused and initiated it.

Thus rebuffed, the envoy sought a private interview with Africanus, according to his orders.
"First of all he told him that the King would
restore his son without a ransom; and then,
as ignorant of the disposition of Scipio as he
was of Roman manners, he promised an immense
weight of gold, and, save for the title of king,
an absolute partnership in the sovereignty—if
through his means Antiochus should obtain
peace." To these advances Scipio replied, " I

am the less surprised that you are ignorant of the Romans in general, and of me, to whom you have been sent, when I see that you do not realise the military situation of the person from whom you come. You ought to have kept Lysimachia to prevent our entering the Chersonese (Gallipoli), or to have opposed us at the Hellespont to hinder our passing into Asia, if you meant to ask peace as from people anxious as to the issue of the war. But after leaving the passage into Asia open, and receiving not only a bridle but a yoke,[1] what negotiation on equal terms is left to you, when you must submit to orders ? I shall consider my son as a very great gift from the generosity of the King. I pray to the gods that my circumstances may never require others ; my mind certainly never will require any. For such an act of generosity to me he shall find me grateful, if for a personal favour he will accept a personal return of gratitude. In my public capacity, I will neither accept from him nor give anything. All that I can give at present is sincere advice. Go, then, and desire him in my name to cease hostilities, and to refuse no terms of peace " (Livy). Polybius's version of the last sentence is a shade

---

[1] Polybius's version is, "having not only submitted to the bridle, but allowed the rider to mount "—and while less graphic it sounds more to the point, and more probable.

different : " In return for his promise in regard
to my son, I will give him a hint which is well
worth the favour he offers me—make any con-
cession, do anything, rather than fight with the
Romans."

This advice had no effect on Antiochus, and
he decided to push on his military preparations,
which were already well in hand. The consular
army then advanced south-east, by way of
Troy, towards Lydia. " They encamped near
the source of the Caicus river, preparing provisions for a rapid march against Antiochus, in
order to crush him before winter should prevent
operations." Antiochus faced them at Thyatira
—modern Akhissar. At this moment, just as
the curtain was about to rise on the final act,
and Scipio reap the reward of his strategy, fate
stepped in. He was laid low by sickness, and had
to be conveyed to Elæa on the coast. Hearing
of this, Antiochus sent an escort to take back
his son to him. This unexpected return of his
son was so great a relief to Scipio's mind as to
hasten his recovery from the illness. To the
escort he said, " Tell the King that I return him
thanks, that at present I can make him no other
return but my advice ; which is, not to come to
an engagement until he hears that I have rejoined
the army "—by this Scipio evidently meant that if
he was in charge Antiochus's life at least was safe.

Although the king had a vast army of sixty-two thousand foot and more than twelve thousand horse, he deemed this advice sufficiently sound to fall back behind the Hermus river, and there at Magnesia—modern Minissa—fortify a strong camp. The consul, however, followed him, and seeing that he refused battle called a council of war. Though the Romans only counted two legions, the equivalent of two allied legions, and some local detachments—about thirty thousand all told,—their verdict was unanimous. "The Romans never despised any enemy so much." However, they did not have to storm his camp, for on the third day, fearing the effect of inaction on the moral of his troops, Antiochus came out to offer battle.

Though the Roman victory was ultimately decisive, they clearly missed the tactical mastery of Africanus, and were even in trouble, if not in jeopardy, for a time. For while the Romans were driving in the enemy's centre, and the mass of their cavalry were attacking the enemy's left flank, Antiochus himself with his right wing cavalry crossed the river—left almost unguarded —and fell on the consul's left flank. The troops there were routed and fled to the camp, and only the resolution of the tribune left in charge rallied them and staved off the danger until reinforcements came. Foiled here and seeing a

heavy concentration developing against him,
Antiochus fled to Sardis, and the survivors of
his broken army followed. Further resistance
was hopeless, his western dominions crumbling
all around him, and the subject States making
their peace with Rome. He therefore retired to
Apamea, and from there sent a peace mission
to the Consul at Sardis, whither Africanus came
from Elæa as soon as he was fit to travel.

Before the mission arrived the terms had
been decided on, and it was agreed that Africanus
should deliver them. " Scipio began by saying
that victory never made the Romans more
severe than before." The conditions were the
same as had been offered before Magnesia,
when the issue was still open ; not a whit augmented because of Antiochus's present helplessness. Antiochus was to retire to the other side
of the Taurus range ; to pay fifteen thousand
Euboic talents towards the expenses of the war,
part at once and the rest in twelve annual instalments, and to hand over twenty selected
hostages as pledge of his good faith. In addition
Antiochus was to give up Hannibal, as it was
" clear that the Romans could never hope to
enjoy peace wherever he was," and certain
other notorious instigators of the war. Hannibal,
however, getting news of this clause, took refuge
in Crete.

The notable feature of these terms, as of those in Africa and Greece, was that the Romans sought security and prosperity merely. So long as Scipio guided Rome's policy, annexation, with all its dangers and troubles, is eschewed. His object is simply to ensure the peaceful predominance of Roman interests and influence, and to secure them against external dangers. It was true grand strategy which, instead of attempting any annexation of Antiochus's normal domains, simply compelled him to retire behind an ideal strategic boundary—the Taurus mountains, and built up a series of sovereign buffer States as a second line of defence between the Taurus range and the Ægean Sea. These were definitely the allies of Rome and not her subjects, and Asia Minor was organised for security by strengthening and rewarding the allies who had been faithful throughout the war. How might the course of history have been changed had not Scipio's successors reversed his policy and entered upon the fateful path of annexation? When the barbarian invasions came they found the Mediterranean world composed of States so thoroughly Romanised that they had long since forgotten the feel of their fetters, yet from this one fact so atrophied as to be a drain and a weakness to Rome. Instead of the ring of virile outposts planned by Scipio, a ring of political eunuchs.

It is an amusing last comment on the settlement with Antiochus, and the removal of the last danger to Rome in the Mediterranean, that on Lucius Scipio's return to Rome " he chose to be called Asiaticus, that he might not be inferior to his brother in point of a surname." He also took steps to ensure that his " triumph " was more splendid in display than that of Africanus over Carthage. The only reward of Africanus was that for a third time he was nominated Prince of the Senate.

CHAPTER XV.

DUSK.

THE moderation and far-sighted policy of Scipio, which had undermined his influence in the years succeeding Zama, was now to cause his political ruin. The sequence of events is somewhat hazy, but their outline is clear. The narrow-minded party, led by Cato, who could not be content with the disarming of the enemy but demanded their destruction, were so chagrined at this fresh peace of mercy and wisdom that they vented their anger on its author. Unable to revoke the peace, they schemed to compass the downfall of Scipio, and fastened on the suggestion of bribery as the most plausible charge. Perhaps, quite honestly, men like Cato could conceive no other cause for generosity to a vanquished foe. However, they seem to have been clever enough not to assail the stronger brother first, but rather, aiming at weakness instead of strength, to strike at Africanus indirectly through his brother.

The first move seems to have been the prosecution of Lucius for misappropriation of the indemnity paid by Antiochus. Africanus was so indignant at the charge that, when his brother was in the act of producing his account books, he took them from him, tore them in pieces, and threw them on the floor of the Senate house. This action was unwise, but very human. Let any one put himself in the place of a man who by unparalleled services had rescued Rome from a deadly menace on her very hearth, and raised her to be the unchallenged and unchallengeable mistress of the world, and then, as he said indignantly, to be called on to account for four million sesterces when through him the treasury had been enriched by two hundred million. We must remember, too, that Scipio was a man suffering from an illness, soon to cause his death, and sick men are inclined to be irritable. Doubtless, too, that supreme self-confidence which marked him developed in later and sickness-ridden years into something approaching arrogance. Thus Polybius tells us that on one occasion, whether this or at the trial later, he bitingly retorted that, " It ill became the Roman people to listen to accusations against Publius Cornelius Scipio, to whom his accusers owed it that they had the power of speech at all." He had refused regal power when it had been thrust upon him, and been content to remain a private citizen, but he expected some measure of special consideration for his supreme services.

The defiant act, however, gave his enemies the opportunity they had longed for. Two tribunes, the Petilii, instigated by Cato, began a prosecution against him for taking a bribe from Antiochus in return for the moderation of his peace terms. The news set all Rome aflame with excitement and discussion. " Men construed this according to their different dispositions ; some did not blame the plebeian tribunes, but the public in general that could suffer such a process to be carried on " (Livy). A frequent remark was that " the two greatest States in the world proved, nearly at the same time, ungrateful to their chief commanders ; but Rome the more ungrateful of the two, because Carthage was subdued when she sent the vanquished Hannibal into exile, whereas Rome, when victorious, was for banishing the conqueror Africanus."

The opposing party argued that no citizen should stand so high as not to be answerable for his conduct, and that it was a salutary tonic that the most powerful should be brought to trial.

When the day appointed for the hearing came, " never was either any other person, or Scipio himself—when consul or censor,—escorted to the

Forum by a larger multitude than he was on that day when he appeared to answer the charge against him." The case opened, the plebeian tribunes sought to offset their lack of any definite evidence by raking up the old imputations about his luxurious Greek habits when in winter quarters in Sicily and about the Locri episode. The voices were those of the Petilii, but the words were clearly Cato's. For Cato had not only been the disciple of Fabius, but himself in Sicily had made the unfounded allegations which the commission of inquiry had refuted. Then after this verbal smoke-cloud, they discharged the poison gas. For want of evidence they pointed to the restoration of his son without ransom, and to the way Antiochus had addressed his peace proposals to Scipio. " He had acted towards the consul, in his province, as dictator, and not as lieutenant. Nor had he gone thither with any other view than it might appear to Greece and Asia, as had long since been the settled conviction of Spain, Gaul, Sicily, and Africa, that he alone was the head and pillar of the Roman power ; that a State which was mistress of the world lay sheltered under the shade of Scipio ; and that his nods were equivalent to decrees of the Senate and orders of the people."

A cloud of words have rarely covered a poorer case, their purpose, as Livy remarks, to " attack

Q

by envy, as much as they can, him out of the reach of dishonour." The pleading having lasted until dusk, the trial was adjourned until next day.

Next morning when the tribunes took their seat and the accused was summoned to reply, the answer was characteristic of the man. No proof was possible either way, and besides being too proud to enter into explanations, he knew they would be wasted on his enemies as on his friends. Therefore, with the last psychological counter-stroke of his career, he achieves a dramatic triumph.

"Tribunes of the people, and you, Romans, on the anniversary of this day I fought a pitched battle in Africa against Hannibal and the Carthaginians, with good fortune and success. As, therefore, it is but decent that a stop be put for this day to litigation and wrangling, I am going straightway to the Capitol, there to return my acknowledgments to Jupiter the supremely great and good, to Juno, Minerva, and the other deities presiding over the Capitol and citadel, and will give them thanks for having, on this day, and at many other times, endowed me both with the will and ability to perform extraordinary services to the commonwealth. Such of you also, Romans, who choose, come with me and beseech the gods that you may have commanders like myself. Since from my seventeenth year until old age, you have always anticipated my years with honour, and I your honours with services."

Thereupon he went up towards the Capitol, and the whole assembly followed; at last, even the clerks and messengers, so that his accusers were left in a deserted forum. "This day was almost more famous owing to the favour of the Romans towards him, and their high estimation of his real greatness, than that on which he rode through Rome in triumph over Syphax and the Carthaginians." "It was, however, the last day that shone with lustre on Publius Scipio. For, as he could foresee nothing but the prosecutions of envy, and continual dispute with the tribunes, the trial being adjourned to a future day, he retired to his estate at Liternum, with a fixed determination not to attend the trial. His spirit was by nature too lofty, and habituated to such an elevated course of fortune, that he did not know how to act the part of an accused person, or stoop to the humble deportment of men pleading their cause " (Livy).

When the adjourned trial took place, and his name was called, Lucius Scipio put forward sickness as the cause for his brother's absence. The prosecuting tribunes refused to admit this, contending that it was merely his habitual disregard of the laws, and reproached the people for following him to the Capitol and for their lack of determination now : " We had resolution enough, when he was at the head of an army and a fleet, to send into Sicily . . . to bring him home, yet we dare not now send to compel him, though a private citizen, to come from his country seat to stand his trial." They failed, however, to carry their point. On Lucius appealing to the other tribunes of the commons, the latter moved that, as the excuse of sickness was pleaded, this should be admitted, and the trial again adjourned. One, however, Tiberius Gracchus, dissented, and the assembly, knowing that there had been friction between him and Scipio, expected a more severe decision. Instead he declared that, " Inasmuch as Lucius Scipio had pleaded sickness in excuse for his brother, that plea appeared to him sufficient; that he would not suffer Publius Scipio to be accused until he returned to Rome, and even then, if Scipio appealed to him, he would support him in refusing to stand his trial. That Publius Scipio, by his great achievements, by the honours received from the Roman people, by the joint consent of gods and men, had risen to such a height of dignity that, were he to stand as a criminal under the rostrum and afford a hearing to the insults of young men, it would reflect more disgrace on the Romans than on him."

Livy adds that Gracchus followed up his decree

by a speech of indignation : " Shall Scipio, the famous conqueror of Africa, stand at your feet —tribunes ? Was it for this he defeated and routed in Spain four of the most distinguished generals of Carthage and their four armies ? Was it for this he took Syphax prisoner, conquered Hannibal, made Carthage tributary to you, and removed Antiochus beyond the Taurus mountains—that he should crouch under two Petilii ? That you should gain the palm of victory over Publius Africanus ? " This speech, as well as his decree, made so strong an impression that the Senate called a special meeting and bestowed the warmest praise on Gracchus " for having consulted the public good in preference to private animosity." The prosecutors met with general hostility, and the prosecution was dropped.

" After that there was silence concerning Africanus. He passed the remainder of his life at Liternum, without a wish to revisit the city, and it is said that when he was dying he ordered his body to be buried there . . . that even his obsequies might not be performed in his ungrateful country."

That he died in voluntary exile at Liternum, probably in 183 B.C., seems assured, but his burial-place is less certain, and monuments of him existed both at Liternum and Rome. At the time of his death he was only fifty-two years of age. By a fitting coincidence his great rival, Hannibal, also died about the same time, and probably in the same year—at the age of sixty-seven. He had escaped, after Magnesia, to Crete, and then taken refuge with Prusias of Bithynia. The Roman Senate had the good sense to realise that it was beneath their dignity to harry him from his last refuge, but the local commander, Flaminius, thought to gain distinction by in-stigating Prusias to murder his trusting guest. Hannibal thereupon defeated the assassins by taking poison.

Even after Scipio's death, his enemies could not rest. It rather " increased the courage of his enemies, the chief of whom was Marcus Porcius Cato, who even during his life was accustomed to sneer at his splendid character." Instigated by Cato, the demand was pressed for an inquiry into the disposal of Antiochus's tribute. Lucius was now the direct target, though his brother's memory was still the indirect. Lucius and several of his lieutenants and staff were arraigned. Judgment was made against them, and when Lucius declared that all the money received by him was in the treasury, and there-fore refused to give security for repayment, he was ordered to prison. His cousin, Publius Scipio Nasica, made a strong and convincing protest, but the prætor declared that he had no

option, in view of the judgment, so long as
Lucius refused repayment. Gracchus again inter-
vened to save his personal enemies from disgrace.
Using his tribunitiary authority, he ordered
Lucius's discharge on account of his services to
Rome, and decreed instead that the prætor
should levy the sum due from Lucius's property.
The prætor thereupon sent to take possession of
it, "and not only did no trace appear of money
received from Antiochus, but the sum realised
by the sale of his property did not even equal
the amount of the fine" (Livy). This convincing
proof of the Scipios' innocence caused a revul-
sion of public feeling, "and the public hatred
which had been directed against the Scipios
recoiled on the prætor, his advisers, and the
accusers."

That his name should have been cleared after
death was, however, no consolation to the last
years of Africanus. "Ingratitude towards their
great men is the mark of strong peoples"—so the
proverb runs. Little wonder that Rome attained
the sovereignty of the ancient world.

CHAPTER XVI.

THERE is perhaps no military dictum so universally quoted as Napoleon's " Read and reread the campaigns of Alexander, Hannibal, Cæsar, Gustavus Adolphus, Turenne, Eugène, and Frederick ; take them for your model, that is the only way of becoming a great captain, to obtain the secrets of the art of war." In another of his maxims he said, " Knowledge of the great operations of war can only be acquired by experience and by the applied study of all the great captains. Gustavus, Turenne, and Frederick, as well as Alexander, Hannibal, and Cæsar, have all acted on the same principles."

Here Napoleon appears to single out a list of six, or possibly seven, commanders who stand out as supreme in the history of warfare. Whether consciously or unconsciously, there has been a general tendency among students of war to accept Napoleon's list as a standard classification of merit—not merely a haphazard mention—when completed by the addition of his own name. True, some have felt the absurdity of counting Eugène as worthy to the exclusion of Marlborough, and others have dropped Turenne because of a perhaps mistaken idea that greatness is synonymous with vastness of destruction, or for the rather better reason that his record lacked the decisive results gained by his compeers. In this way one finds that not a few commentators have arrived at a list of three ancient commanders—Alexander, Hannibal, and Cæsar—and three modern—Gustavus, Frederick, and Napoleon—as the Himalayan peaks of military history. That Frederick, with his gross blunders and most unoriginal " oblique order," should receive preference over such consummate artists as Turenne and Marlborough must remain one of the mysteries of military criticism. This is not the place to deal with the fallacy. Here we are concerned with the great captains of the ancient world, and so far as we desire a comparison with the modern, Napoleon himself affords it, since his supremacy is hardly questioned.

Let us therefore compare Scipio with these three ancient great captains, by a threefold study and test—as general, as man, and as statesman. Any such comparison must be based on the conditions these men had to deal with, and on the skill with which they turned these conditions to their advantage.

Alexander, and to a hardly less degree Cæsar, enjoyed the immense asset of having autocratic power, complete control over the forces and resources available. Even Hannibal, if poorly supported, was immune from the petty interference with his operations against which Scipio, like Marlborough later, had to contend.

Alexander's victories were won over Asiatic hordes, whose lack of tactical order and method offset their numerical superiority, and as Napoleon demonstrated in his well-known comment on the Mamelukes, the defects of Asiatic troops increased in ratio with their numbers. No critic places Clive in the first rank of great captains, and but for the clear brilliance of his manoeuvres and the scale of his conquests Alexander would suffer a like discount. Cæsar, also, was hardly more than an able " sepoy general " until Ilerda and Pharsalus, and, as he himself is said to have remarked, he went " to Spain to fight an army without a general, and thence to the East to fight a general without an army." And even so, Cæsar found himself, owing to an unwise dispersion of force, twice forced to fight under the handicap of inferior strength. In the first, at Dyrrhacium, he suffered defeat, and though he atoned for it at Pharsalus, this single first-class victory is a slender base on which to build a claim to supreme generalship.

But if we are to accept Napoleon's dictum that "in war it is not men but the man who counts," the most significant fact is that both Alexander and Cæsar had their path smoothed for them by the feebleness and ignorance of the commanders who opposed them. Only Hannibal, like Scipio, fought consistently against trained generals, and even as between these the advantage of conditions is on Hannibal's side. For his three decisive victories—the Trebia, Trasimene, and Cannæ—were won over generals not only headstrong and rash, but foolishly disdainful of any tactics which savoured of craft rather than of honest bludgeon work. Hannibal knew this well—witness his remark to the troops who were to lie concealed for the flank attack at the Trebia, "You have an enemy blind to such arts of war." Flaminius and Varro were mental Beefeaters, and their names are instinctively bracketed in history with those of Tallard, Daun, Beaulieu, and MacMahon. Hannibal taught the Romans the art, as distinct from the mechanism, of war, and once they had profited by his instruction his successes were limited. Marcellus and Nero were capable of winning tricks off him, and if they could not take a rubber neither could Hannibal. But in surveying Scipio's record, not only do we find his tactical success unchequered, but that his opponents from the outset were generals trained in the Barcine school, and all the evidence goes to show that Hannibal's brothers, Hasdrubal and Mago, were no mean commanders.   And the apex of Scipio's career, Zama, is unique in history as the only battle where one acknowledged great captain has, on his own, defeated another decisively.

Thus if conditions, and the extent to which they are not only met but turned to advantage, be the test, Scipio's pre-eminence is clear.

If the quality of a general's art be the test, universal opinion concedes that Hannibal excelled Alexander and Cæsar.   Alexander's victories were rather triumphs of method, calculations working out with straightforward precision, but unmarked by any subtle variations and traps for the enemy.   In Alexander, for all his greatness, still lingered traces of the Homeric hero, the glorification of the physical elements at the expense of the mental.   It was this knight-errantry which led him to stake his life so often in the forefront of the battle, needlessly risking thereby the collapse of his plans and the lives of his army.   To him might well be applied the rebuke made by Timotheus to Chares, when the former remarked : " How greatly ashamed I was at the siege of Samos when a bolt fell near me ; I felt I was behaving more like an impetuous youth than like a general in command of so large a force." This mistaken Bayardism, too, explains the absence of the subtler artistry in his battles—it is epitomised in his rejection of Parmenio's proposal to attack Darius by night at Arbela, on the ground that he would not " steal a victory." Cæsar's plans were assuredly more difficult to guess, but he did not "mystify, mislead, and surprise " to anything like the degree that Hannibal attained. So general is the recognition of Hannibal's genius in this battle art that he is commonly termed the supreme tactician of history. Yet in ruse and strategem the record of Scipio's battles is even richer. Recall the unfortified front, the timing of the direct assault, and the lagoon manœuvre at Cartagena ; the double envelopment and reversal of adverse ground conditions at Bæcula. The change of hour and of dispositions, the refused centre, the double oblique, and the double convergent flank blows at Ilipa. As Colonel Denison notes in his ' History of Cavalry,' Ilipa is " generally considered to be the highest development of tactical skill in the history of Roman arms." I would suggest that the student of war, if he considers it as a whole—from the mental opening moves to the physical end of the pursuit,—cannot but regard it as without a peer in all history.

Continuing, observe the use of ground first to counter his enemy's numbers and then to force him to fight separated battles, as well as the wide turning movement, against Andobales. Watch Scipio luring on his enemy into the ambush at Salæca; study his masterpiece in firing the Bagradas camps—the feint at Utica, the sounding of the evening call, the timing of and distinction between the two attacks, and the subtlety with which he gains possession of the main obstacle, the gates of the Carthaginian camp, without a struggle. Note, later, his novel use of his second and third lines as a mobile reserve for envelopment at the Great Plains, and the chameleon-like quickness with which he translates his art into the naval realm when he frustrates the attack on his fleet. Finally, at Zama, where he is confronted with an opponent proof against the more obvious if more brilliant stratagems, we see his transcendent psychological and tactical judgment in his more careful but subtly effective moves—the "lanes" in his formation, and the synchronised trumpet blast to counter the elephants; the deliberate "calling off" of the *hastati ;* the calculated change of dispositions by which he overlaps Hannibal's third, and main, line ; the pause by which he gains time for the return of his cavalry, and their decisive blow in Hannibal's rear.

Is there such another collection of gems of military art in all history ? Can even Hannibal show such originality and variety of surprise ? Moreover, if Hannibal's " collection " in open battle is somewhat less full than Scipio's, in two other essentials it is bare. Even his devoted biographers admit that siegecraft, as with Frederick, was his weakness, and he has nothing to set off against Scipio's storm of Cartagena, which, weighed by its difficulties, its calculated daring and skill, and its celerity, has no parallel ancient or modern.

The other and more serious void in Hannibal's record is his failure to complete and exploit his victories by pursuit. Nowhere does he show a strategic pursuit, and the lack of even a tactical pursuit after the Trebia and Cannæ is almost unaccountable. In contrast we have Scipio's swift and relentless pursuit after Ilipa, and hardly less after the battle on the Great Plains— which alike for range and decisiveness are unapproached until Napoleon, if then. In ancient times Scipio has but one possible rival, Alexander, and in his case there was repeatedly an interregnum between the tactical and the strategic pursuit, which caused a distinct debit against his economy of force. For his turning aside after Issus a strategic argument can be made out, but for his delay after Granicus and Arbela there appears no cogent reason save possibly that of distance—the fact at least remains that his campaigns offer no pursuit so sustained and complete as that down the Bætis, or Guadalquiver. It may be suggested that Scipio did not always pursue as after the two battles cited. But an examination of his other battles show that pursuit was usually either rash or unnecessary—rash after Bæcula, where he had two fresh armies converging on him, and unnecessary after Zama, where there was no enemy left to be a danger.

From tactics we pass to strategy, and here a preliminary demarcation and definition may simplify the task of forming a judgment. Strategy is too often considered to comprise merely military factors, to the overshadowing of the political and economic, with which it is interwoven. The fallacy has been responsible for incalculable damage to the fabric of warring nations. When such critics speak of strategy, they are thinking almost solely of logistical strategy—the combination in time, space, and force of the military pieces on the chessboard of war. Between logistical strategy and chess there is a distinct analogy. But on a higher plane, and with a far wider scope, is grand strategy, which has been defined as " the transmission of power in all its forms in order to maintain policy." " While strategy is more particularly concerned with the movement of armed masses, grand strategy, including these movements, embraces the motive forces which lie behind them, material and psychological. . . . The grand strategist we see is, consequently, also a politician and a diplomatist." [1]

As a logistical strategist Napoleon is unrivalled in history—save possibly by the Mongol, Subutai, from what we can piece together of the scanty records of his campaigns. The ancients suffer, in common with the modern precursors of Napoleon, the handicap that the organisation of armies in their day did not permit of the manifold combinations that he effected, a handicap which persisted until the divisional system was born in the late eighteenth century, beginning with De Broglie. Previously we find detachments, or occasionally, as in Nero's classic move to the Metaurus against Hasdrubal, a two-army combination, but the scope and variation of such combination were inevitably narrow until armies came to be organised in self-contained and independent strategic parts—the modern division or army corps—just in time for the genius of Napoleon to exploit these new possibilities. But within the inherent limitations of pre-Napoleonic times, Scipio develops a range of strategical moves which, it may be fairly claimed, is unequalled

[1] 'Reformation of War,' by J. F. C. Fuller.

R

in the ancient world.   The hawk-like swoop on
Cartagena, so calculated that none of the three
Carthaginian armies could succour their base in
time.   The hardly less bold and calculated blow
at Hasdrubal Barca before either Hasdrubal
Gisco or Mago could effect a junction—how closely
the margin of time worked out we know from
Polybius.   Nor is there any doubt whether these
strategic moves were deliberate, as in many
ascribed to ancient commanders on supposition
by military critics who view old theatres of war
through modern spectacles.   Polybius and Livy
both tell us that these calculations were in Scipio's
mind.   Again, the way in which Scipio stood
guard over Hasdrubal Gisco while his detachment under Silanus moved and fell on Hanno
and Mago before they had word of his approach.
Swift as the march, as thorough was the defeat.

Next, the master move leading to Ilipa,
whereby his direction of advance cut Hasdrubal
and Mago off from their line of communication
with Gades, which in the event of their defeat
meant that retreat to their fortified base was
barred by the river Bætis (Guadalquiver).   The
upshot showed both the truth of his calculation
and the proof of the fact—the result was the
annihilation of the Carthaginian armies.   This
seems the first clear example in history of a
blow against the strategic flank.   Here is born

the truth which Napoleon was to crystallise in his cardinal maxim that " the important secret of war is to make oneself master of the communications." Its initiation is sometimes claimed for Issus, but at best Alexander's manœuvre was on the battlefield, not in strategic approach, while the simple explanation is that the sea prevented a move on the other flank and that the bend in the river Pinarus dictated the direction of it.

Admittedly Scipio's strategic intention at Ilipa is a hypothesis, and not definitely stated in Livy or Polybius; but the established facts of the advance, and still more of its sequel, form a chain of indirect evidence that could not be firmer. Even Dodge, one of Scipio's consistent detractors, emphasises this threat to the strategic flank.

Before passing on to his African campaigns, we may note Scipio's anticipation of, and trap for Hannibal at Locri. Then note how, on landing in Africa, his first care is to gain a secure base of operations, fulfilling the principle of security before he passes to the offensive. See him baulk the enemy's superior concentration of strength by the " Torres Vedras " lines near Utica. Note the rapidity with which he strikes at Hasdrubal and Syphax at the Great Plain, before their new levies can be organised and consolidated, and how in the sequel he once more stands guard, this time over Carthage, while his detachment under Lælius and Masinissa knocks Syphax out of the war. Finally, there is his move up the Bagradas Valley by which he simultaneously compels Hannibal to follow, and facilitates his own junction with Masinissa's reinforcement from Numidia. So complete is his mastery on the strategical chessboard that he even selects the battlefield most favourable to the qualities of his own tactical instrument. Then, Zama decided, he pounces on Carthage before the citizens can rally from the moral shock.

What, if any, mistakes can be set down on the debit side of his strategy? A study of military commentaries shows that his critics advance but three—that Hasdrubal Barca and Mago in turn escaped from Spain, and that Scipio did not lay siege to Carthage immediately on landing in Africa. The obvious reply is to ask how many times did Darius, a far more vital personal factor, escape Alexander, why Cæsar let slip Pompey after Pharsalus, or Hannibal fail to move on Rome after Trasimene or Cannæ— there were far less adequate reasons. But apart from the extreme difficulty of catching an individual without an army, it is hoped that the earlier chapters may have disposed of these empty criticisms. Even after Bæcula, Scipio was still markedly inferior in strength to the Carthaginian forces in Spain, and further, Hasdrubal was only able to elude Scipio's watch and cross the Pyrenees with so weak a contingent that he was forced to recruit in Gaul for two years before he could advance on Italy. Mago's escape was still more an individualistic effort. As for the question of an immediate advance on Carthage, Scipio would have been an impetuous fool, not a general, if he had laid siege to so vast a fortified city as Carthage with the small original force that he carried into Africa. The clearest proof of his wisdom in first seeking a secure base of operations lies in the overwhelming enemy concentration from which he only escaped by his foresight in forming his " Torres Vedras " lines.

In Alexander's record even his modern biographers do not suggest any notable examples of logistical strategy, apart from certain swift marches such as that from Pelium on Thebes. There are no combinations or checks to enemy combination. His strength lies in his grand strategy, of which we shall speak later.

With Hannibal, too, his logistical strategy is mainly a matter of direct marches and of admirable care to secure his communications, apart from the very disputable purpose of his move on the line of the Po which, in effect, separated the elder Scipio from Sempronius, his fellow-consul; and secondly, his feint at Rome in the attempt to relieve the pressure on his allies at Capua, which, though clearly intended, was abortive. Against these must be set, first, the fact that the advantage of his hazardous march over the Alps was foiled of its purpose by the elder Scipio's quicker return from the Rhone by the Riviera route; second, the fact that he failed to prevent the junction of Sempronius with Scipio on the Trebia. Later, there are, among other indisputable failures, the neglect to exploit Cannæ even by the seizure of Canusium, let alone a thrust at Rome; the times his moves were parried by Fabius and Marcellus; Nero's brilliant deception by which Hannibal remained stationary and in the dark, while his brother was being crushed on the Metaurus. Finally, we see him outmanœuvred by Scipio in the preliminary moves before Zama. Outstandingly great as a tactician, Hannibal is not impressive as a strategist; less so, indeed, than several of Scipio's forerunners among the Roman generals.

Cæsar, in contrast, stands out more in logistical strategy than in tactics. But classic as are many of his moves in Gaul one has to remember that they were made against barbarians, not trained generals such as those with whom Scipio, Hannibal, Nero, and Marcellus had to contend.

Against Pompey's lieutenants in Spain he extricated himself with surpassing skill from a critical position, into which perhaps he should not have got. Then in Greece he threw away his superiority of force by dispersion, and suffered a severe defeat at Dyrrhacium, nearly disastrous as he confessed when he said : " To-day the victory had been the enemy's, had there been any one among them to gain it." His retreat was a masterly feat, if we overlook the quality of his opponents, but later he failed in his attempt to prevent the junction of Pompey and Scipio Nasica, and had to fight at Pharsalus without his detachments against a concentrated force. That his tactics turned the balance does not affect the reflection on his strategy.

If Scipio, then, may be given the palm for logistical strategy among the ancients, how does he compare with Napoleon ? We could adopt the historical argument that a man must be judged by the conditions and tools of his time, pointing out not only the indivisible organisation with which Scipio had to work, but that he was a pioneer where Napoleon had the experience of ages to build on. But we prefer rather to abandon this sound and normal test, which inevitably negatives true comparison, and admit frankly Napoleon's supremacy in this sphere. The scales are amply balanced by Scipio's superiority as a tactician. By wellnigh universal opinion Napoleon's tactics were below his strategical level, and it is this compensating factor which has led military criticism to bracket Hannibal with Napoleon among the great captains—a factor which we suggest applies still more in Scipio's favour compared with Napoleon.

From logistical strategy we come to grand strategy. This lies in the domain of peace as much as in war, and hence for simplicity it may be well to deal with the grand strategy which contributed to the winning of wars, and reserve for our study of Scipio as statesman that part of his grand strategy which had its goal in the subsequent peace.

If our examination of the years 210-190 B.C. has achieved its historical purpose, it should be clear that Scipio showed an understanding of war in its three spheres—mental, moral, and physical, and of their interplay, such as is just dawning on the most progressive politico-military thought of to-day. Further, he translated this understanding into effective action in a way that we may possibly achieve in the next great war— more probably, we shall be fortunate to get out of the physical rut by 2000 A.D.

For proof of this claim look at the progressive and co-ordinated steps by which, starting from the valley in Rome's darkest hour, he climbs steadily and surely upwards to the summit of his aims, and plants Rome's flag on the sunlit peaks of earthly power. Scipio is a mountaineer, not a mere athlete of war. The vision that selects his line of approach, and the diplomatic gifts which enable him to surmount obstacles, are for him what rock-craft is to a climber. His realisation of the importance of securing his base for each fresh advance is his snow-craft, and his employment of military force his ice-axe.

Watch him, on arrival in Spain, make wide inquiries about the position of the Carthaginian forces, and the importance and topography of Cartagena. His genius tells him that here is the base and pivot of the Carthaginian power in Spain, and shows him the feasibility, the way, and the effect of such a stroke—at the moral and economic rather than the purely military objective.

Cartagena gained, note the wisdom which by conciliating the citizens secures his acquisition against internal treachery, and further enables him to economise the garrison by converting the citizens into active partners in the defence. What a diplomatic coup is the prompt release and care of the Spanish hostages. If Napoleon's presence was worth an army corps, Scipio's diplomacy was literally worth two. It converted allies of the enemy into allies of his own.

There was grand strategy, too, in his wise restraint from a further advance, in order to allow the moral and political effect of Cartagena and its sequel to develop. Thus Hasdrubal Barca, seeing the Spanish sand trickling fast from his end of the hour-glass to Scipio's, was drawn into the offensive move which enabled Scipio to beat him before the other Carthaginian armies came up. Once more victory paves the way for diplomacy, as that in turn will pave the way for further victories. He sends home the Spanish captives without ransom, and, still more shrewdly, returns Masinissa's nephew loaded with presents—surely never in history has the money invested in presents brought a greater ultimate dividend.

Next, note the rapidity with which Scipio nips in the bud the incipient threat from Hanno, and in contrast the constraint by which he avoids wasting his force on a number of petty sieges which could bring no commensurate profit. The wider effect of Scipio's action in Spain also deserves notice, for Livy tells us that this year Hannibal in Italy was for the first time reduced to inaction, because he received no supplies from home owing to Carthage being more anxious about the retention of Spain.

Scipio's grand strategy was from now onwards to lift the pressure off Rome in ever-increasing degree. His success in Spain compelled the Carthaginians to invest there the forces that might have been decisive in Italy, and at Ilipa he wipes them off the military balance-sheet.

The instant that victory in Spain is sure, and before turning to the mere clearing operations, his grand strategical eye focusses itself on Africa. His daring visit to Syphax, his meeting with and despatch of Masinissa to Numidia—here are two strings to a bow which shall soon loose a shaft at the heart of Carthage. For an object-lesson in the selection of the true objective, and its unswerving maintenance in face of all obstacles and perils, the next few years are a beacon light for all time. He schemes, he prepares, he works unceasingly towards the goal. The military interference of the enemy is almost the least of his difficulties. Sexual passion frustrates one of his shrewdest diplomatic moves, but his plan is too flexible, too well conceived, for even this blow to have more than a transient effect. Jealous rivals, short-sighted politicians, military " die-hards " do their best, or worst, to block his plan, and failing in this, to obstruct him and curtail his strength. He builds and trains a fresh army out of adventurers and disgraced troops. Yet he never makes a rash or a false move, mindful always of the principle of security. By diplomacy again he creates in Sicily a sure source of supply.

He sends a reconnoitring expedition to clear up the African situation, and appreciating Masinissa's material weakness, refuses to be rushed into a move before his own weapon is forged. When he lands, his first efforts are directed to gain a secure base of operations. And gauging exactly the strength and weakness of Carthage and of his own position, he adapts consummately his immediate end to his existing means. Each successive move is so directed as to subtract from the military and political credit of Carthage and transfer the balance to his own account. His restraint when this ultimate goal is so close in mileage, though not in reality, is almost miraculous in a commander so youthful and so early successful. But he has long realised that Syphax and Masinissa are the two props of the Carthaginian power in Africa, and before he attempts to turn this power out of its seat his first aim is to upset its stability, by taking away one prop and knocking away the other. Just as he has gained this end, passion once more intervenes to threaten his military achievement as it previously thwarted his diplomacy, but the psychological master-move by which he foils Sophonisba's wiles averts the danger.

Now assured of security he aims at Carthage itself, and characteristically pauses in sight of Carthage to achieve, if possible, the supreme economy of force of a moral victory instead of the drain of a physical siege. The move succeeds, and Carthage capitulates with Hannibal still across the seas, helpless to aid. And when by a gross breach of faith the treaty is violated, Scipio is not caught off his guard. By a fresh and rapid series of moves, a perfect combination of military, economic, and psychological pieces, he achieves the checkmate in a brief span of time. Is there anything in history which for continuity of policy, combination of forces— material and moral,—and completeness of attainment can compare with it ? Scipio is the embodiment of grand strategy, as his campaigns are the supreme example in history of its meaning.

Alexander certainly preceded Scipio as the first grand strategist, but without arguing the question how far his moral and economic action was fortuitous rather than marked by the exquisite calculation of Scipio's, his task was much simpler, and as a despot he had none of Scipio's internal obstacles to surmount. It is, above all, because of the close parallel with modern conditions, political and organic, that Scipio's grand strategy is so living a study for us to-day.

Alexander's achievements may have excelled Scipio's in scale—not really so much, for if Alexander established for himself an empire from the Danube to the Indus, which collapsed on his death, Scipio built for Rome an empire which stretched from the Atlantic to the Black Sea and the Taurus mountains—an empire which endured and increased. And whereas Alexander built on the foundations laid by Philip, Scipio came on the scene at a moment when the very foundations of Roman power in Italy were shaken by a foreign foe. There are grave blemishes, too, on Alexander's strategy—while he was consolidating his offensive base in Asia Minor, he was in acute danger of losing his home base in Europe. By the disbandment of his fleet he exposed the European coasts to the superior Persian fleet, and Darius's one able commander, Memnon, seized the chance to raise Greece, where the embers of discontent smouldered in Alexander's rear. Only Memnon's death saved Alexander from disaster, and gained time for him to carry out his plan of crippling Persian sea power by land attack on their naval bases. Again, by lack of strategical reconnaissance, Alexander blundered past the army of Darius, lying in wait in northern Syria, which moved down and cut his communications, a danger from which he only saved himself, facing about, by tactical victory at Issus. It is well to contrast this with Scipio's thorough strategical reconnaissance and search for information before every move. If Alexander's grand strategy has a narrow advantage by the test of quantity, Scipio's is clearly superior in quality.

In the comparison of Scipio with Napoleon, if the latter's superiority in logistical strategy is recognised, we have to set against this both his tactical and his grand strategical inferiority. As a grand strategist Napoleon's claims are marred not only by his failure to realise the aim of grand strategy—a prosperous and secure peace,—but by his several blunders over the psychology of his opponents, over the political and economic effects of his actions, and in the extravagant later use of his forces and resources.

Finally, let us point out that while Alexander had the military foundations laid by Philip to build on, while Hannibal built on Hamilcar, Cæsar on Marius, Napoleon on Carnot—Scipio had to rebuild on disaster.

From the comparison of generalship we pass to the comparison of character. Here, to enumerate at length the qualities which distinguished Scipio as a man would be wearisome. His moderation, his self-control, his human sympathy, his charm of manner, his magnetic influence over troops—shared by all the greatest captains,—his exaltation of spirit, these have shone through his deeds and speeches. Of his private life we know little save by inference. He married Æmilia, daughter of the consul

Æmilius Paullus who fell at Cannæ, the marriage apparently taking place after his return from Spain and before his departure for Africa.

From the solitary anecdote or two which survive, the marriage seems to have been a happy one, and Scipio to have shown more deference to his wife's opinion than was common at the time. That she had tastes too expensive for Cato's liking seems assured ; she was probably one of those leaders of Roman female society against whom he directed his complaints— that by wearing " a garment of various colours, or riding in a carriage drawn by horses " in the towns, they would undermine the social fabric and create discontent. The indulgence shown by Scipio to his wife, and his breach with tradition in treating her better than his slave, was certainly one of the factors which rankled in Cato's mind. Of the moral influence distilled in the Scipio family life, the best proof is an indirect one. Their daughter Cornelia was given in marriage to Tiberius Gracchus, apparently after he had so generously defended Scipio's reputation, and was the mother of the Gracchi. The way in which she carried out their education, and the principles with which she inspired these future reformers, make one of history's noblest pages.

Outside the domestic sphere, Scipio's influence

on social history rests on his love for and in-
troduction of Greek literature and philosophy.
" A man of great intellectual culture," he could
speak and write Greek as well as he could Latin—
he is said to have written his own memoirs in
Greek. To his Greek studies he clearly owed
that philosophy of life which permeates all his
recorded acts and sayings. He seems to have
taken the best elements from Greece and Rome,
and to have blended them—refining the crudeness
and narrowness of early republican Rome without
diminishing its virility. So marked was his
influence that he may, with some justice, be
termed the founder of Roman *civilisation*. " To
him is attributed the rise of manners, the origin
of their taste for propriety, and of their love of
letters." A rather touching instance of his own
love of letters is enshrined in his friendship and
admiration for the poet Ennius, a regard so
profound that he left orders that after his death
a bust of the poet should be placed with his in
the tomb of the Scipios. Yet it was this very
influence as an apostle of civilisation and of the
humanities that earned him the bitter animosity,
as it stimulated the fear, of Romans of the old
school. Cato and his kind might have forgiven
his military success and his self-confidence, but
nothing but his downfall could atone for his
crime in introducing Greek customs, philosophy,

S

and literature. It is not unlikely that this damaged him, and undermined his influence even more than his contempt for pettier minds and his moderation to conquered foes. These are the only charges which his enemies could bring against his character, and in this fact lies perhaps the strongest proof of his superior moral nobility. For the malice of an enemy will fasten on any conceivable weakness, and thus the charges levied against a great man form a standard of moral measure which is one of the best of comparisons.

From this test Scipio alone of the great captains of antiquity emerges scatheless of any charge that suggests a definite moral blemish. It is true that we can discount most of the charges brought against Hannibal—impiety, avarice, perfidy, and cruelty beyond the customs of his day. But Alexander, whatever allowance we make in other accusations, stands convicted of want of self-control, violent outbursts of temper and prejudice, cruel injustice as to Parmenio, ambitious egotism verging on megalomania, and ruffianism in his cups. Alexander was tarred with the brush of Achilles.

Similarly, Cæsar's many great qualities cannot disguise his sexual license, his political corruption and intrigue, and the predominantly selfish motives which inspired his work and achieve-

ments. There are interesting parallels between
the careers of Cæsar and Scipio. Compare
Cæsar gaining the province of Gaul by intrigue
and threat, Scipio the province of Spain at the
call of his country in the hour of adversity.
Compare Cæsar forming and training an army
for the conquest of Rome, Scipio for the sal-
vation of Rome from her foreign foes. Compare
Cæsar crossing the Rubicon, Scipio the Bagradas
—and their objects. Compare Cæsar receiving
the honour of a triumph over fellow-Romans,
Scipio over Syphax and Hannibal. Lastly, if
it be true that " a man can be known by the
friends he keeps," compare Catiline with Lælius
and Ennius. Napoleon's saying that " Laurels
are no longer so when covered with the blood of
citizens," comes curiously from his lips. For
Napoleon's ambition drained the blood of France
as surely as Cæsar's spilt the blood of Rome.
It would suffice to strip the laurels from the brows
of both, and enhance the contrast with Scipio,
the supreme economist of blood and of force
in the selfless service of his country. It is not
difficult to guess why Napoleon should ignore
Scipio in his list of military models !

By any moral test Scipio is unique among the
greater captains, possessing a greatness and
purity of soul which we might anticipate, not
necessarily find, among the leaders of philosophy

or religion, but hardly among the world's supreme men of action. The clergyman who, a century ago, was Scipio's one English biographer, and whose work suffers by its brevity, its historical slips and the omission of all study of Scipio as a soldier, had yet one flash of rare insight and epigrammatic genius when he said that Scipio was "greater than the greatest of bad men, and better than the reputed best of good ones."

Last of all we turn to Scipio as statesman— that part of his grand strategy which lies definitely in the state of peace. The Abbé Seran de la Tour, who compiled a life of Scipio in 1739, dedicated it to Louis XV., and in his dedication wrote : "A king has only to take for his model the greatest man by far in the whole of Roman history, Scipio Africanus. Heaven itself seems to have formed this particular hero to mark out to the rulers of this world the art of governing with justice." The lesson, we are afraid, was lost on Louis XV., a man who at the council table "opened his mouth, said little, and thought not at all," whose life is as full of vulgar vice as it is bare of higher aims. We suspect the Abbé of a capacity for subtle sarcasm.

When Scipio came on the stage of history, Rome's power did not even extend over the whole of Italy and Sicily, and this narrow territorial sway was gravely menaced by the encroachments, and still more the presence, of Hannibal. At Scipio's death Rome was the unchallenged mistress of the whole Mediterranean world, without a single possible rival on the horizon. This period saw by far the greatest expansion in the whole of Roman history, and it was due either directly to Scipio's action, or made possible by him. But if territorially he stands out as the founder of the Roman Empire, politically his aim was not the absorption but the control of other Mediterranean races. He followed, but enlarged, the old Roman policy, his purpose not to establish a centralised, a despotic empire, but a confederation with a head, in which Rome should have the political and commercial supremacy, and over which her will should be paramount. Here lies the close parallel with modern conditions, which gives to the study of his policy a peculiar and vital interest. Cæsar's work paved the way for the decline and fall of Roman power. Scipio's work made possible a world community of virile States, acknowledging the overlordship of Rome, but retaining the independent internal organs necessary for the nourishment and continued life of the body politic. Had his successors possessed but a tithe of the wisdom and vision of Scipio, the Roman Empire might have taken a course analogous to that of the modern

British Empire, and by the creation of a ring of semi - independent and healthy buffer States around the heart of Roman power, the barbarian invasions might have been thwarted, the course of history changed, and the progress of civilisation have escaped a thousand years of coma and nearly as much of convalescence.

His peace terms alone would place Scipio on a pinnacle among the world's great conquerors— his entire absence of vindictiveness, his masterly insurance of military security with a minimum of hardship to the conquered, his strict avoidance of annexation of any civilised State. They left no festering sores of revenge or injury, and so prepared the way for the conversion of enemies into real allies, effective props of the Roman power. In the meaning of Scipio's name—a " staff "—was epitomised his grand strategy in war and peace.

The character of his policy was in tune with his character as a man, disdaining the tinsel glory of annexation as of kingship, for the solid gold of beneficent leadership. Scipio laboured for the good and greatness of Rome, but he was no narrow patriot, instead a true world statesman. The distinction between Scipio and Cæsar has been crystallised in the phrase, " Zama gave the world to Rome, Pharsalus gave it to Cæsar," but even this does not render Scipio full justice, for he could look beyond the greatness of Rome's glory to the greatness of her services to humanity. Not an internationalist, he was a supra-nationalist in the widest and best sense.

Attila was called the " scourge of the world," and with a difference only in degree most of the great captains, from Hannibal to Napoleon, have had no higher objective conception than to thrash their enemies, or at best their country's enemies, into submission. Thus this fallacy paved the way for a reaction equally short-sighted, which led Green, in his ' History of the English People,' to write : " It is a reproach of historians that they have turned history into a mere history of the butchery of men by their fellow-men," and to follow this up by the absurd declaration that " war plays a small part in the real story of European nations." So arose a very large modern school of historians who sought, irrationally, to write history without mentioning, let alone studying, war. To ignore the influence of war as a world-force is to divorce history from science, and to turn it into a fairy tale. The grand strategy of Scipio is a signpost pointing the true path of historical study. Scipio could administer military beatings at least as effectively and brilliantly as any other of the greater captains, but he saw beyond the beating to its object. His genius revealed to him that peace and war are the two wheels on which the world runs, and he supplied a pole or axle which should link and control the two to ensure an onward and co-ordinated progress. Scipio's claim to eternal fame is that he was the staff, not the whip, of Rome and of the world.

BIBLIOGRAPHY.

AFTER due reflection and discussion with others, I have decided not to litter the actual pages of the book with footnote references, but to list the various historical sources in this bibliographical appendix. The modern fashion tends to treat an historical study as a literary card-index rather than as a book to be read, and in many instances this tendency is carried so far that the footnotes swamp the text. Experience suggests that even the barest footnote reference is a distraction to the reader's eye, and momentarily dams the flow of the narrative through his mind. For this reason I have omitted references from the actual pages except where they could be woven into the text, and if some readers hold that I err in this decision, I can at least plead that I do so in good company.

The ancient sources—all of which, except Polybius, require to be treated with critical caution—have been :—

Polybius, X. 2-20, 34-40 ; XI. 20-33 ; XIV. 1-10 ; XV. 1-19 ; XVI. 23 ; XXI. 4-25 ; XXIII. 14.

Livy, XXI.-XXII., XXV.-XXXIX.

Appian, *Punica, Hisp., Hann., Syr.*

Aulus Gellius, IV. 18.

Cornelius Nepos, XXXI.-XXXII. ; *Cato; Hannibal.*

Plutarch, *Cato; Æmilius Paullus; Tib. Gracchus.*

Valerius Maximus, III. 7.

T